THE
MORAL
LEADER

The London Lectures in Contemporary Christianity

This is an annual series of lectures founded in 1974 to promote Christian thought about contemporary issues. Their aim is to expound an aspect of historical biblical Christianity and to relate it to a contemporary issue in the church in the world. They seek to be scholarly in content yet popular enough in appeal and style to attract the educated public; and to present each topic in such a way as to be of interest to the widest possible audience as well as to the Christian public.

Recent lectures:

1994 'Transforming Leadership: A Christian approach to managing organizations', *Richard Higginson*

1995 'The Spirit of the Age', *Roy McCloughry*

1996 'The Word on the Box: Christians in the media', *Justin Philips, Graham Mytton, Alan Rogers, Robert McLeish, Tim Dean*

1997 'Matters of Life and Death: Contemporary medical dilemmas in the light of the Christian faith', *Professor John Wyatt* (published by IVP in 1998 as *Matters of Life and Death: Today's healthcare dilemmas in the light of Christian faith*)

1998 'Endless Conflict or Empty Tolerance: The Christian response to a multi-faith world', *Dr Vinoth Ramachandra* (published by IVP in 1999 as *Faiths in Conflict: Christian integrity in a multicultural world*)

2000 'The Incomparable Christ: Celebrating his millennial birth', *John Stott*

2001 'Moral Leadership', *Bishop James Jones* (published by IVP in 2002 as *The Moral Leader: For the church and the world*)

2002 'Moving Genes: Evolving Promise or Un-natural Selection?', *John Bryant*

The London Lectures Trust

The London Lectures in Contemporary Christianity are organized by the London Lectures Trust, which was established as a charity in 1994. The committee represents several different evangelical organizations.

THE
MORAL
LEADER

For the church and the world

JAMES JONES
WITH ANDREW GODDARD

Based on the AD 2001 London Lectures
in Contemporary Christianity

Inter-Varsity Press

INTER-VARSITY PRESS
38 De Montfort Street, Leicester LE1 7GP, England
Email: ivp@uccf.org.uk   Website: www.ivpbooks.com

First published 2002

British Library Cataloguing in Publication Data
A catalogue record for this book is available from the British Library.

ISBN 0–85111–283–8

Set in Adobe Garamond 11/14pt
Typeset in Great Britain by CRB Associates, Reepham, Norfolk
Printed and bound in Great Britain by Creative Print and Design (Wales),
Ebbw Vale

*Inter-Varsity Press is the publishing division of the Universities and Colleges
Christian Fellowship (formerly the Inter-Varsity Fellowship), a student movement
linking Christian Unions in universities and colleges throughout Great Britain,
and a member movement of the International Fellowship of Evangelical Students.
For more information about local and national activities write to UCCF,
38 De Montfort Street, Leicester LE1 7GP, email us at email@uccf.org.uk, or
visit the UCCF website at www.uccf.org.uk.*

Contents

Preface

This book is a treble conversation. It is a conversation between two Christians, between a bishop and a lecturer in ethics. It is a correspondence between Andrew and me, begun when I responded to an invitation to give the 2001 London Lectures on Moral Leadership. Shortly after the lecture series I went on study leave back to the theological college where I trained and whose Council I now chair. Perchance I found that the room I was given was on the same corridor and exactly opposite Andrew's!

The conversation between us is within the evangelical tradition that has nurtured us both. It is the evangelical tradition of Cranmer and Wilberforce and not of the parodied transatlantic tele-evangelists! It is a noble tradition within the European Church that has shaped and continues to shape the church in England. Evangelicalism at its best is stereophonic, listening to both the Word and the world. It is moreover a conversation between the Word and the world. These pages and our dialogue are definitely set within that second conversation.

As our conversation reveals, we are not without disagreement! Indeed, reading Andrew's erudite responses to my lectures made me feel again something of that furrowed brow when you get your essays back after being marked by your tutor. At least Andrew has spared me a publishing of a grade. That is left to the reader!

Andrew's responses stimulated and encouraged me. I resisted the temptation to answer his responses to each chapter: bishops are too often perceived as wanting to have the last word. What we both would like is for this, the third conversation, to continue with you the reader.

Evangelicalism is often seen today by its critics as a closed system that forecloses dialogue and argument. The renaissance of the evangelical tradition within the Church of England and the Anglican Communion and the flourishing of community churches and ethnic churches with a distinct evangelical and charismatic emphasis presents evangelicals and the church at large with a fresh challenge to understand and learn from one another. We hope that this book will help evangelicals move beyond our ghettos and enable those of other traditions to take seriously the evangelical contribution to church and society.

The Rt Revd James Jones
Bishop of Liverpool
July 2002

1

TAKE ME
TO YOUR (MORAL) LEADER

INTRODUCTION
by Claire Curtis-Thomas MP

The best lack all conviction, while the worst
Are filled with passionate intensity.

These words from W. B. Yeats's 'The Second Coming' speak to us uncomfortably of one of the dilemmas of recent decades. He was writing at the time of the Irish rising, but the observation is timeless: that, faced with the challenge of evil, good men are uncertain as to what to do, while 'the worst' – the Hitlers, the Stalins, the Pol Pots and so many more – know all too well what they believe and will stop at nothing to put their beliefs into action.

'Take me to your (moral) leader' is Bishop James's theme in this first chapter, and it reflects both upon the vacuum of moral leadership that seems to exist and at the same time upon the perceived need for something to fill that vacuum: to provide some sort of certainty, something or someone to look up to.

Political leaders have always been dangerous role-models.

History records the names of those who, filled with that passionate intensity, were sure that their way was the only way: that their vision was the one that must be imposed on the world. Such absolute and dangerous conviction starts wars, opens up political divides, and sets nations, tribes and religions against one another. Yeats's observation is made the more poignant by his own identification with the cause of Irish nationalism. Of the 1916 rising he memorably declared that 'a terrible beauty is born'; he said of those who died for the Republican cause that 'an excess of love / Bewildered them till they died'. Today, as the hard-won peace process in Ireland struggles for survival, nationalist and political proclamations still seem far from providing a coherent and lasting answer.

For those of us with faith, the answer lies, as it has always lain, in the Christian gospel and Christ's imperative of peace. Here again there is an irony: our age, understandably wary of institutional dogma, looks askance at authority in any form, elevating the cult of the individual in the elusive pursuit of happiness. Thus the baby is thrown out with the bathwater, and the Christian faith, Philip Larkin's 'vast motheaten brocade', is seen as part of the failed past obsessed with its wealth, its fading power and its falling numbers; it is rejected, and its prophetic voice all too often unheard or ignored.

But James's encounters with young people, as recounted in this chapter, and the message of concern and involvement coming from those same young people, must offer hope and a way forward. Uncluttered by dogma, and surprisingly and refreshingly untouched by received ideas and the siren songs of consumerism, they are concerned for the world they are inheriting and have the potential to affect it for the better. Those who are involved with the young, as teachers, mentors and guides, know their responsibility and the privilege it brings; exposure to the idealism and vision of so many of today's young people is an inspiring antidote to the illnesses of our age. Another poet, John Milton, painted a picture of a fallen society where 'the hungry sheep look up, and are not fed'. It is for the moral leaders of every faith, and even of none, to offer that sustenance, and thus to provide for our future.

TAKE ME
TO YOUR (MORAL) LEADER
by James Jones

The changing social context

Since September 2001 we have witnessed some significant events which seem to have changed the landscape, or at least affected the light in which we now view the scene. The terrorist attacks in America have been talked about in apocalyptic language. They raise fundamental issues about leadership in the modern world. How do political and religious leaders hold together the principles of justice and mercy in the pursuit of freedom and peace?

The race riots in Oldham earlier in the same year exposed some of the inherent instabilities of modern Britain. Among many issues to be faced are those of leadership, especially by those who hold positions of responsibility within the faith communities.

The prospect of human cloning comes ever nearer, with doctors such as Severino Antinori breaking ranks with colleagues and announcing publicly his plans to proceed with the first ever cloning of a human baby. Here is an episode of modern science that raises the question: who exercises leadership, both within the scientific community and in the world at large?

Then we are increasingly aware of the damage that we are inflicting upon the planet with our reckless exploitation of its finite resources. Hard-won agreement on various protocols seems to be falling apart. Discord about the environment makes the future even more precarious, and again poses the question: who can or will offer leadership on behalf of the whole earth?

the spiritual and the moral are as important as the economic and physical aspects of regeneration

While the planet is under threat both from our irresponsible attitude to the environment and from the terrorist attacks of extremists, there is a widespread feeling that the very ground of our communities is being shaken by a social earthquake. Robert Putman, in his book *Bowling Alone: The Collapse and Revival of American Community*,[1] suggests that we are exhausting our social capital. His thinking is influential in shaping that of Prime Minister Tony Blair. Anxieties about the community's deficit seem to be opening up new possibilities, so that the British Government is creating even more opportunities for faith communities to be engaged in the State's social and educational provision. This is highly contentious.

On the one hand, the faith communities are responding enthusiastically to these initiatives, arguing that they need to be partners in the regenerating of society because the spiritual and the moral are as important as the economic and physical aspects of regeneration. On the other hand, this is bitterly opposed by philosophers such as A. C. Grayling. He believes strongly that the State should disengage from the faith communities, whose beliefs, he maintains, are fundamentally irreconcilable. He fears that embracing the faith communities into the State's social provision will ultimately institutionalize division within society. Sharpening the focus of this debate is the Government's White Paper on education, which gives strong affirmation to the involvement of not just the churches, but all faith communities, in the State provision of education.

Thirty years ago I trained as a teacher. If any of us students had predicted then that in thirty years' time the State would be offering the church a greater stake in education, we would have been laughed out of the tutorial. It is a fascinating feature of our so-called post-Christian society that the Christian church's contribution to education is being not only sought but positively affirmed and encouraged.

In his address to the Christian Socialist Movement on 29 March 2001, entitled 'Faith in Politics', Tony Blair spoke unequivocally:

> Church schools are a true partnership between the churches and the Government. They are a pillar of our national education system valued by very many parents for their faith character, their moral emphasis and the high quality of education they generally provide.

But his position has been strongly criticized by Bill Morris, General Secretary of the Trades Union Congress, who, like Grayling, fears that schools that are faith-based will fuel sectarianism in society.

Faith schools point to both the opportunity and the obstacles that Christians face in the modern world. Their presence indicates that our culture, while apparently open to spirituality, refuses to attach greater credibility to one religion than to another. In this context, the exercise of leadership, moral and spiritual, presents challenges that may leave us feeling that we are in a unique situation in the history of the church's engagement with human society. Lessons from the past are not only poor masters for the future, but inexperienced servants too! All these issues have come into much sharper focus since September 2001.

In a concise and perceptive essay in *Crucible*, entitled 'Whither Anglican Social Ethics?',[2] Alan M. Suggate discerns some of the major shifts in the social context of the last fifty years. These have profoundly shaped the ethical debate. Society has undoubtedly become more plural, which means that 'the Church of England has to struggle harder to receive a hearing and sustain a public theology'.[3] Suggate adds that social policy has deposed certain assumptions about the person-in-society, social justice and welfare, in favour of the freedom and responsibility of individuals and families. As someone closely involved in urban renewal programmes, I wrestle all the time with these changing assumptions, which are expressed by both politicians and civil servants as they formulate and execute public policy on community regeneration.

Suggate also draws attention to the fact that there is now a greater international awareness: 'Global capitalism imperiously both homogenises and fragments, provoking resistance from pressurised cultures and people.'[4] (He wrote this before that fateful 11 September!) This very different world that we now inhabit calls for the emergence of international moral leadership, the like of which we have never yet seen. Furthermore, offering leadership in a globalized world cannot be done without the media, which project leaders in ways that raise problems of their own. More will be said on this later.

Leaders with a mission

The story goes that while William Gladstone was felling a tree, news came that Queen Victoria was inviting him to form his first administration. He opened the message from the courier, muttered, 'Very significant!' and continued to fell the tree! Having completed the arboreal task, and in his shirtsleeves, he pronounced these famous words: 'My mission is to pacify Ireland.'

These sentiments were remarkable, not because, over a century later, that process has yet to come to fruition, but because very few prime ministers would have described any of their tasks in the language of mission. Yet, for Gladstone, both his public office and his private life were characterized by imperatives that were explicitly both spiritual and moral. In an interview for the *Sunday Telegraph*, the present prime minister, Tony Blair, spoke openly and yet with reticence about the spiritual and moral foundations of his own political outlook. In particular, he spoke of the shift in his views from utilitarianism to natural law:

> I'm far more of a believer in the power and the necessity to make judgements about the human condition, as opposed to simply saying, well look, what's good for the greatest number is fine. I'm a great respecter of science, and the ability of science to inform our perceptions of the world. But I think there is a danger sometimes that we look at everything just in terms of what its utilitarian value is.[5]

Although utilitarianism is the most popular frame of morality today (the interviewer continues), the Prime Minister has rumbled its inadequacies. 'The greatest happiness for the greatest number' is a fine principle when that consists of building more and better schools and hospitals. But it is inadequate to the task of framing a moral position to withstand a policy of, say, ethnic cleansing.

Commenting on the interview, Matthew d'Ancona compared Blair and Gladstone as two prime ministers who could be ranked together, not only because of their political ambition to settle the Irish question, but also on account of the moral and theological convictions underpinning their political philosophy and pragmatism.[6]

If ever a political dilemma called for moral as well as political leadership, it is in Northern Ireland, where, as I write, the peace process flounders. It is salutary to remind ourselves of the influence for good that was the legacy of the elected representatives from Ireland when they joined the British Parliament in 1804. Their entrance revived the hope of the abolitionists of the slave trade, and later secured a majority in the House of Commons for the abolition of that trade.[7] The Rev. Thomas Price, in his review of the life of William Wilberforce, notes that the Irish MPs were generally free of the commercial interests of the English MPs, who, on the grounds of economic ruin, resisted both the abolition of the slave trade and the end of slavery.[8] William Wilberforce, who had the ability to become prime minister, yielded up the opportunity of high office in the Cabinet because he was possessed of the moral conviction that slavery was evil. He was tenacious of the moral principle, and brooked no opposition from those who warned that if he persisted he would 'ruin the Empire'. He was a politician whose ambitions were theologically and ethically rooted in the Bible. Here was a moral leader.

Here is a flavour of Wilberforce's rhetoric:

> It is another capital excellence of Christianity that she values moral attainments at a far higher rate than intellectual acquisitions, and proposes to conduct her followers to the heights of virtue rather than of knowledge.[9]

He compares Christianity favourably with the systems of antiquity:

> Many of the philosophers spoke out, and professed to keep the lower orders in ignorance for the general good; plainly suggesting that the bulk of mankind was to be considered as almost of an inferior species. Aristotle himself countenanced this opinion. An opposite mode of proceeding naturally belongs to Christianity, which without distinction professes an equal regard for all human beings, and which was characterised by her first promulgator as the messenger of 'glad tidings to the poor'.[10]

The nineteenth century opened with Wilberforce's moral and political triumph, the abolition of the slave trade and slavery, and closed with Gladstone's explicitly moral agenda. The decades in between saw some of the most radical social reform ever witnessed in Britain, from the Parliamentary Reform Bill to the Factory Acts. It was a very different period from the century we now inhabit at the beginning of the third millennium. Even though the proposed reforms were sometimes fiercely opposed, the pugilists fought their good fights within a clearly defined ring. And even though some had begun to think in ways that would redefine the philosophical boundaries for ever, an ethical settlement of Christian principles held sway. By virtue of its empire, Britain was exposed to a variety of other beliefs; yet there was such a confidence in the superiority of its own systems that it would take more than a century for the supremacy of Christianity to feel the cold shower of pluralism.

It is tempting and misleading for Christians to ache nostalgically for this bygone age when moral absolutes seemed as firm as the iron railings to which the suffragettes chained themselves. There were blind spots in the moral vision of the nineteenth century. The rightful emancipation of women began in the century that also saw the undermining of Christianity's pre-eminence. Indeed, some feminist commentators would argue that it was the very undermining of the dominance of Christianity that opened up the liberation of women.

We do well to be cautious in thinking that the grass must have been greener on the other side of the twentieth century. The satirist P. J. O'Rourke suggests one word as a corrective for all those who want to go back in time to some mythical golden era. Just remember one word: 'Dentistry!'

The task ahead

I deliberately begin these reflections with such recognition because, in the current debate about spiritual and moral values in public life, Christians are either perceived as, or accused of, wanting to turn the clock back and to put the moral genie back in the bottle. They do not notice – it is thought – that the bottle is already shattered into a myriad cultural shards. In this book I want to chart a way forward that is consonant with the virtues of the past and that takes us into the future. I hope to demonstrate that, just as St Paul found common ground with the moral and philosophical leaders in the Areopagus at Athens, so there are new bridges to be built between our richly diverse culture of sub-cultures (or, as Jonathan Sacks, the Chief Rabbi, has described Britain, our 'community of communities') and the moral essence of Christianity.

In this first chapter we shall observe some of the shifts in moral outlook around us today. In the second, we shall explore how, and at what points, this moral maze might connect with our understanding of the kingdom of God. In the third, I will take courage and suggest, by reference to Paul's evangelism in Athens, how Christianity might speak the language of moral conviction into a diverse and pluralistic culture. The final chapter will attempt to draw from Jesus those qualities that might characterize those who either aspire to, or have projected on to them, the responsibilities of moral leadership.

As I contemplate this outline I confess to questioning my wisdom in undertaking such an enterprise. I am neither politician, nor philosopher, nor moral theologian. The more I have read on these issues, the less adequate to the task I have felt. I am but a jobbing bishop, a pastor who is both learning and teaching, and the discipline of marshalling the ideas in this book has been of great benefit to me personally.

The cultural tripod

'Me personally.' In today's world, it appears that, if something may benefit an individual personally without at the same time inflicting harm on another, it is deemed morally acceptable. Individualism has been elevated to the status of a moral principle. This is a reduced form of utilitarianism, in which the principle of 'the greatest happiness for the greatest number' translates into 'the greatest happiness for the individual, so long as the greatest happiness for the greatest number of other individuals is left unaffected by the action'. Paul Vallely, in his book *New Politics*,[11] provides an excellent treatise on the contemporary relevance of Catholic social teaching. He summarizes the condition of 'modern man': 'confined to the language of individualism [he] has lost the ability to make moral sense of his life and takes refuge in a world view which celebrates consumerism, the freedom of the individual and a blind faith in science'.[12]

This tripod – consumerism, the freedom of the individual, and faith in science – supports the edifice of modern life in the West. And those who find themselves in leadership, whether sought or thrust upon them, secure their own position by appealing to, encouraging and reinforcing these blind beliefs. It is not without significance that advertising agencies, which arose out of the commercial need to sell products, are now used to sell the offerings of political parties. The merging of products and politics into a seamless marketing exercise is the ultimate genuflection at the altar of consumerism and individualism.

individualism has been elevated to the status of a moral principle

But this modern scenario is not without its own contradiction, as Robin Gill skilfully points out in his book *Moral Leadership*.[13] He salutes the publication of the 1993 papal encyclical *Veritatis Splendor* and applauds Pope John Paul II for his exposé of the contradiction 'that in the secular world individual conscience and autonomy have become ever more important at precisely the moment when genetic and social determinism have also become predominant'.[14] Gill wishes that the Pope had gone further to expose the inconsistency. The moral relativism that is the hetero-doxy of postmodernism requires us to believe that there are no moral absolutes.

The moral relativists see persons as products of social condi-tioning. And here there is a touch of irony. In a consumer society dedicated to the freedom and autonomy of the individual, where choice and the freedom to choose whichever product suits are elevated to the point of authenticating our very existence, we ourselves are no more than products of social conditioning! Social determinism means that there is no absolute right or wrong. We believe and make our choices – economic or moral – according to the society in which we have been conditioned and determined. This is a bleak picture. It means that, when we see an old lady trying to cross the street, there is no objective difference between our helping her across or knocking her down. There is, of course, a difference for the old lady – but a purely subjective one. There is no moral objectivity that binds others to her in some sort of obligation and responsibility. Whichever action was chosen sprang from a process of conditioning and determinism. This argument, pushed to its logical conclusion, has all sorts of repercussions for public policy and moral leadership, not least in relation to the criminal justice system, the treatment of offenders and the nature of punishment.

In her book *Metaphysics as a Guide to Morals*, Iris Murdoch writes, 'Just (proper) deterrence, rehabilitation and retribution are the three bases of a political theory of punishment, and most fundamental of these is retribution.'[15] Yet it is precisely the retributive element about which people today are less sure. Deterrence, reformation and the protection of society form the triangle in which people feel most comfortable. But, as C. S. Lewis remarked in his essay *The Abolition of Man*,[16] if you take the retributive element out of punishment, what right does any of us have to subject another person to reform and transformation if he or she does not in some sense deserve it? To evacuate from the debate about punishment all mention of moral objectivity is to abandon all notion of desert and retribution at the same time.

Signs of moral hope?

Despite the evidence of society's slippage into moral relativism and the autonomy of the individual, I want to begin to swim against the tide of other commentators and suggest that popular culture is not totally devoid of objective moral principles. Two episodes in particular suggest that the moral vaults of our culture are not entirely bankrupt of the capital of ethical absolutes.

nobody said that apartheid was relatively wrong

The first concerns the overthrow of apartheid in South Africa. When the world community acted in concert against this sovereign nation, forcing her to change her internal structures and abolish apartheid, nobody protested that this was an unacceptable violation of her integrity as an independent State. In the furious and sometimes violent debate about apartheid and racism, neither those on the left, nor the forces of liberalism, argued that morality was simply a product of social determinism – that whether or not you thought that black and white were equal depended on how your society had been conditioned. Nobody said that apartheid was *relatively* wrong (although those on the right who advocated a softly-softly approach did give the impression that apartheid was tolerably wrong; that is, a wrong that could be tolerated in an evolving process of social change).

The world community eventually spoke and acted decisively,

declaring apartheid *absolutely* wrong. South Africa was forced to change. What was it that opened the door of Nelson Mandela's cell in the prison on Robben Island? It was the the world community's intuiting of an absolute moral value that all men and women are equal, regardless of race, colour or creed.

Of course, there were many factors that brought about change, internal as well as external, economic and political as well as ethical. But the point is that in the moral debate at the end of the twentieth century, which supposedly had given birth to moral relativism, there was no reference to the autonomy of the individual and to the importance of choice. Instead, we saw the elevation of a moral principle of social justice, beneath which autonomous individualism was decisively subjected. And rightly so.

One factor in this process was the Anglican Church under the leadership of Archbishop Desmond Tutu. While living in solidarity with the disadvantaged, he enabled others to trace backwards from their moral intuition to the God who had spoken through the historic deliverance of his people, and supremely in the just and merciful Jesus. And although it was probably a popular subscription to the utilitarian ethic of the greatest happiness for the greatest number that won the day (the blacks constitute the greatest number in South Africa), the principle of utilitarianism did in this instance offer insight into, and access to, an absolute and universal value. But I emphasize my point: the voice of social determinism and moral relativism was strangely silent at the end of the twentieth century.

The second episode is closer to home for me. During the six weeks of Lent 2000, I visited fourteen secondary schools and colleges of further education and met with literally thousands of sixteen- to eighteen-year-olds. I asked if I could meet with sixth-formers to hear their dreams and dreads, their longings and their loathings about the future millennium. I asked too if I could tell them why I thought that Jesus Christ was relevant 2,000 years on. To stimulate the discussion, we produced three video clips – on the future of the planet, on relationships and on the spiritual quest. I asked the young people to indicate on a scale of 0 to 10 how worried they were about the future of the planet. In each venue, on each occasion, 100% placed themselves between 5 and 10. I then asked the ethical question, whether we ought to do something about the future: 99% of them felt that we should, placing themselves between 5 and 10.

This encounter with thousands of young people impressed on me the moral absolutism of their views. When we explored the source of their moral conviction, it was found to range from enlightened self-interest (with one young man believing in reincarnation and wanting to ensure a decent environment for his rebirth), to a clear sense of duty to future generations. In a chapter on ecology and the environment in his book *What is Mission?*,[17] Andrew Kirk writes about seeing the Earth not so much as something we have on trust but as something we actually borrow from future generations. He quotes the African proverb 'We have borrowed the present from our children.'[18] I found this attitude prevalent among the young people I listened to.

I do not deny that environmentalism is the new indoctrination promulgated in schools today. I for one am happy with that doctrine, although I have to confess that, along with the rest of the church, I have been slow to embrace the moral and theological imperative of caring for the environment. The prophetic voice has been heard from outside the walls of the church. With this example it is important to signal that, when it comes to moral leadership, the church has sometimes been the audience and not the prophet. But the point of my findings is that our society, especially its young people, manifests a moral conviction that is not totally explicable in terms of the tripod of consumerism, autonomy of the individual and blind faith in science.

The sense of duty towards future generations challenges the god of consumerism by restraining exploitation and unsustainability. It checks the autonomy of the individual by confronting the god of choice with the needs of others. And it resists blind faith in science by questioning the gods of the laboratory who genetically modify our food and clone our pets and maybe even yet our babies.

In Kantian terms, the ethical aspirations of young people sound like categorical imperatives. There is a moral duty to care for the environment. It is not just about doing something in order to achieve certain outcomes, which would render it a hypothetical imperative. We ought to live in a responsible and careful relationship with the environment because that is both how it is and how it ought to be.

Morality and the media

But from where does such intuition derive? That is for a future chapter. For now, I simply want to reiterate that there is evidence, especially (thank God) among young people, that the cultural cupboard is not bare and, in fact, is being replenished with moral principles. Schools play their parts and so do the media, which create the public world in which we all live and move and have our being. The media are relevant to the theme of moral leadership because there is no leadership without followership, and there can be no following without communication and communion. It is the media that create the context for both moral debate and moral leadership in the modern world.

Because our imaginations are engaged and stimulated by drama and conflict, the media, especially television, know how to secure an audience. They present the world to us – indeed interpret the world for us – in terms of opposites. Sociologists of the media call this the binary meaning of television: issues are polarized between left and right, Arab and Jew, black and white, unions and management, 'wet' and 'dry', Christian and Muslim. The drama and conflict that flow from these contrasting opinions make exciting programmes that engage the audience and establish the all-important ratings.

There are two ways of viewing this method. On the one hand,

we could regard it as just a form of classical discussion, the famous dialectic in which we seek to arrive at the truth through the cut and thrust and counter-thrust of argument. On the other hand, we might despair at the reduction of important moral and political ideas into even more extreme opposites, where subtlety and nuance for ever give way to megaphonic soundbites.

Today's moral leaders usually have about twenty seconds in which to articulate their opinion. They may have taken an hour to deliver a lecture. They may have been given five minutes in the studio to engage in a dialectical interview with John Humphrys or Jeremy Paxman. Then an editor will choose about twenty seconds from either the former or the latter. That clip will be played and replayed on news bulletins, and upon it the audience will form its judgments. The Press will then go to someone famous for an opposite view, and an article based on the Titans' clash of soundbites will appear. Finally, the insatiable Internet will gobble up such morsels for infinity.

there is no leadership without followership

My youngest daughter rushed up to me recently to declare that there were 4,100 pages on the internet all about me.

'How do I get them off?' I begged.

'You can't!' she chirped as she rushed back to surf the Net.

My heart sank as I imagined people unknown to me logging on to find out my moral opinions. 'Take me to your moral leader,' they will command their voice-activated laptop. And where will the server take them? Such is the new world in which moral leaders are now framed and the debate about morality is now conducted by email and SMS.

RESPONSE
by Andrew Goddard

The pace of moral change

One of the major challenges faced by moral leaders today is the rapidly changing context. The 2001 race riots in Oldham now seem like old and distant news. Such fundamental moral questions as racism light up our television screens briefly, when they become explosive, but then easily drift from our national consciousness and risk being left unaddressed until the next explosion occurs.

Human cloning has been back in the news, with the pressing question of therapeutic (rather than reproductive) cloning, and the House of Lords' approval of stem-cell research. We have witnessed strong exchanges between Christian leaders who take fundamentally opposed views on this moral issue. Is this a positive development that brings hope to many who are suffering, or is our willingness to create and experiment on human embryos another frightening sign of what Pope John Paul II has called 'a culture of death', which 'the gospel of life' must challenge?[19] As I write these words, that debate too has largely disappeared from the news, although doubtless it will resurface again soon in some form or another.

This constantly changing, high-profile media debate about moral issues is what comes to people's minds when they think about moral leadership today. Perhaps one of the greatest strengths of this chapter (and those that follow) is that James has resisted what must at times have been the strong temptation to let varied and complex moral issues such as these set the agenda. He has not simply responded to the desire for the church to provide moral leadership by speaking out on particular areas of moral concern. Instead, as someone who often does speak out in the media and in his regular preaching and other public ministry, he has sought to step back from the coalface and take stock of this aspect of his calling.

Such 'theological reflection' is an increasingly important component in the training of future church leaders. While the academic expertise in such traditional disciplines as biblical studies, doctrine, church history, liturgy and ethics remains vital, it cannot stay on a theoretical level, divorced from practice and from the contemporary context of the church and its mission. This first chapter has helpfully set the present in the context of the past, and subsequent chapters promise to develop the fundamental biblical and theological rationale for moral leaders in church and nation at the start of the twenty-first century.

In response, I initially want to address the key words in the chapter title: 'your (moral) leader'. Then I shall turn to the chapter's analysis of the context in which moral leadership is sought and offered.

Who is the moral leader?

My primary concern lies in the ambiguity of the central concept of the chapter title, that of the idea of the *moral* leader. As the examples in the chapter illustrate, this can be understood in a number of different ways. Three in particular seem important.

First, it can refer to the moral qualities of any person in any form of leadership. These are matters of *character and conduct* on the part of leaders in any sphere of life. Here we are thinking of a moral leader in contrast to an immoral leader. That concern may focus on matters of what we class as 'private life', such as the sexual conduct of those in leadership. Sadly, that is often where it tends to get focused, as the British Conservative Government of the mid-1990s learnt when it launched its 'Back to Basics' campaign. More directly relevant are issues of character and conduct that have a direct bearing on the sphere in which the leader offers leadership. How significant is it if a Cabinet minister is untruthful about her activities in the department she heads, or if a leading businessman is involved in shredding documents that implicate his firm in shady deals?

Secondly, the term 'moral leader' could also refer to the *commitment and convictions* of those in positions of leadership. Perhaps the contrast here is with a non-moral, technocratic leader. In our political world, where, in reality, so much is governed by bureaucracy, technology and the mass media, Gladstone's sound-bite 'My mission is to pacify Ireland' is wonderfully inspiring, and it is interesting that we still look for moral leaders in this mould to inspire us politically. Whether it is Margaret Thatcher, with her (in)famous citation of St Francis on becoming prime minister in 1979, or Tony Blair in his creation of New Labour, leaders with such commitment and moral and theological convictions underpinning their political philosophy are the ones who seem attractive.

Thirdly, the designation 'moral leader' can also be given to those whose sphere of *competence and concern* is that which we call 'morality'. He or she may be someone who is seen as in some sense having authority to address ethical issues, whether matters of personal or of social morality. Alternatively, he or she may be someone whose own conduct enables him or her to give a moral lead on how we should live our lives. Such people may be leaders in other spheres of life – financial or political leaders, or leaders in education or the trade unions. This chapter has cited the Member of Parliament William Wilberforce and his moral leadership in relation to the slave trade. More recently, one thinks, for example, of the way Bob Geldof used his prominence in the music world to provide a moral lead in the relief of famine through Band Aid.

Often, however, moral leaders in this sense are not already recognized leaders. The novelist, columnist and broadcaster Anne Atkins rose to prominence by taking a moral stand on a particular issue and then found her opinions sought on a whole range of moral questions. In terms of personal moral example, there are those who are marked out as moral leaders because of their response to a crisis in their own lives or the life of their community. Many moral leaders in this sense are able to escape the public media gaze, and we can all think of parents, neighbours, teachers, work colleagues and others whose exemplary lives and wise counsel have shaped us morally. Sometimes, however, this happens on a wider scale. One example is Gordon Wilson, whose offer of forgiveness to the IRA, after they had killed his daughter and many others at Enniskillen, marked him out as a moral leader.

These three types of moral leader are certainly not mutually exclusive. They often go together, and, indeed, they are regularly expected to be combined in any 'moral leader'. As a result, some in leadership are wary of appearing to be moral leaders in either of the last two senses, lest their own personal moral failings are then subject to scrutiny. I shall return to this later in discussion of the media.

Given these different senses of 'moral leader', a crucial issue is how they relate to Christian leadership in society and leadership in the church. It is clear, for example from the Pastoral Epistles, that those who exercise leadership within the church are expected to be 'moral leaders' in the first sense, of being people of good conduct and character (e.g. 1 Tim. 3:1–13). It should also, of course, be the case that Christian leaders are men and women marked out by their conviction and commitment to the gospel. For many in wider society, however, these two characteristics of moral leadership are of little significance unless, sadly, a Christian leader falls from grace.

The attention is focused more on the third category. Church leaders and Christians in other contexts are looked to for leadership when something is understood as a 'moral issue'. This is, I think, the primary sense in which James is using the term. Church leaders are often called upon to provide moral comment on issues of the day. To my mind, this raises not only great opportunities but also dangers. One of these is the danger of 'moralism', in which Christian leaders are understood to be telling people how to live, what to do and what not to do, rather than proclaiming the good news of God in Christ and explaining how to live lives worthy of this gospel.

Whose moral leader?

A related danger is raised by the other keyword in this chapter's title: 'your'.

Many may understand the chapter title as a personal address in the singular. As James points out, in the current moral climate 'individualism has been elevated to the status of a moral principle'. On this interpretation, the reader is being invited to identify whom he or she has personally chosen to be his or her own individual moral leader. Knowing James's strong critique of such an individualistic, self-directing understanding of moral leaders, and the value he places on leading communities, I am sure that this meaning was not intended. But, once a plural rather than a singular understanding of 'your' is given priority, the groups being addressed need to be more explicitly identified. They could be distinguished in all sorts of ways. For example, those of an older generation perhaps still look to the head of State as their moral leader, but this appears to be much less the case among younger people. Another distinction is the one drawn in this chapter between faith communities (in general) and secular society. Given the importance of schools in moral formation, it is unsurprising that education policy is proving to be a major area of dispute. Some look for a universal, national, non-religious system, while others welcome and encourage institutional diversity that reflects the different religious and moral communities in society today.

While that difference between 'faith communities' and secular society is obviously important and shapes the discussion in the nation at large, perhaps the most important distinction from a Christian perspective is that between the church and the world. Here the approach implied in the chapter title could lead to two difficulties. One is that 'moral leader' perhaps does and should refer to something significantly different when that language is used in the church as distinct from the world. If that is so, we must be clear about what the differences are.

The other difficulty arises when we turn the question around and think about those *for whom* someone is acting as a moral leader. The title contains hidden within it some major questions about how the Christian moral leader speaks when fulfilling the third role of moral leader and pronouncing on moral issues. In particular, the people we understand to be represented by that little word 'your' might prove to be decisive to a Christian moral leader thinking about whether, 'when the church contributes to public debate on matters of concern to secular society at large, it should forget that it is the church of Jesus Christ and should address society on terms common to all participants' (Oliver O'Donovan's summary of a view he rejects but sees as sadly common in the Church of England).[20]

Idols of our time

Whether the 'you' of the title is to be focused on the Christian community or on wider society, the fact remains that all of us live in 'the world', in the sense in which John's Gospel uses that term to speak of creation broken from God and hence in darkness and rebellion against him. One of the most important tasks for Christian witness is therefore to understand the world and the modern forms of brokenness, darkness and rebellion; I would disagree with very little in this chapter's powerful account. In particular, I think it is not overstating the current situation to speak of a context in which the exercising of leadership, moral and spiritual, presents challenges that leave many of us feeling that we are in *a unique situation in the history of the church's engagement with human society*, and to warn against (often false) nostalgia on the part of the church.

Paul Vallely's tripod of consumerism, individual freedom and faith in science is indeed something to which moral leaders apparently have to appeal. I would want to extend this analysis in a number of ways. The chapter not only offers a sociological analysis of our contemporary context but in fact unveils the idols of our time, the 'wisdom of this age ... [and] the rulers of this age, who are coming to nothing' (1 Cor. 2:6) and some of the current forms of 'the rulers ... authorities ... the powers of this dark world ... the spiritual forces of evil in the heavenly realms' (Eph. 6:12). In a time in which many people think they have come of age and that the biblical condemnations of idolatry have little relevance because we no longer bow down before statues, this discernment is a crucial part of the calling of moral leaders. Before I suggest some additional features of our moral landscape, this use of the language of idolatry and its significance for moral leaders needs further unpacking.

Much debate takes place about whether religion is necessary for morality. Many people rightly highlight the moral failures of religious people and point out the goodness of those who profess no faith in God. Some, such as Anthony Grayling, almost turn the issue on its head and worry about the bad influence of faith communities on national moral life. What such debates can often miss, however, is that we are all fundamentally religious people. How we live our lives and how we think about morality – as individuals, families, neighbourhoods, nations and the church – are therefore shaped by our religious convictions. Paul's account in the opening chapter of Romans is quite clear that all that is wrong in human society is ultimately to be traced back to the rejection of the one true God and to the decision to worship and serve idols instead. In the words of Bob Dylan, we discover that all human beings 'gotta serve somebody'. That, of course, is why worship is central in Christian moral formation.

> *we are all fundamentally religious people*

Why does such a perspective seem strange to so many today, given that for so much of history the link between religious worship and morality was not disputed? Perhaps it is in part because of the idols this chapter identifies. These not only shape so many areas of our lives and determine what a convincing moral argument is; they have also reconfigured how we understand morality and hence moral leadership. These idols therefore easily prevent us from seeing what is really involved in moral thinking and decision-making.

As the chapter implies, our *consumerist* mindset means that we can view moral decision-making as if we were consumers in a supermarket of moral opinions and moral issues. So we travel down the sex aisle, and choose whether to buy a traditional 'sex only in heterosexual marriage' product or one of the newer range of goods on prominent display (and probably on special offer). Then we move on to the medical aisle, where there is an ever-expanding range of produce we are encouraged to sample.

Some of it is quite expensive, and some perhaps not to our taste, but clearly popular with other customers, who see medicine as simply another product to enable them to maximize and satisfy their desires.

As in our real supermarket shopping, we sadly fail to see that behind each product on offer is a whole process that we need to consider. As a result, we do not grasp the truth that real moral thinking is not about distinct, unrelated choices, but about a vision of human life as a whole. It is a story we are telling ourselves about who we are, through our relationships with the rest of creation, our fellow humans and God. The specific moral choices we make, therefore, actually reveal the deeper, spiritual and religious choices we have made, even if only subconsciously, and even if the choices reveal a lack of coherence and integration in our polytheistic, postmodern culture.

real moral thinking is ... about a vision of human life as a whole

Our emphasis on *individual freedom* fuels this reconception of morality and its separation from worship and religion. It leads, as the chapter describes, to a form of moral privatization and moral relativism. As with consumerism, we are led to focus on decisions and dilemmas rather than on issues of character formation and the kinds of people we should be, a perspective more clearly related to religion and spirituality.

What is more, by emphasizing the freedom of the individual we fail to see how morality is, at heart, about community and tradition. Since the Enlightenment, in part because of the historic authoritarianism and failures of the Christian church, there has been a rebellion against having our lives shaped by historic traditions and contemporary communities. This is part of the problem facing moral leaders today. Many people have no place for them, as they seem to threaten personal freedom; while those who do look for moral leadership often want to be consumers who choose their own leader, preferably one who is not going to make awkward demands on their lives. And yet it is our culture and our communities and their leaders that from childhood onwards shape our moral lives. Talk of the individual and his or her freedom can make sense of morality only when set in this wider context.

Our *faith in science* also, I believe, contributes to our failure to understand morality. But it is really only a subset of a much more significant cultural commitment to technology and the quest for technical solutions. This modern idol, which the great French thinker Jacques Ellul called 'Technique', is marked by its quest for mastery, control and efficiency in every area of life, and its influence on our lives and thinking runs much wider and deeper than 'science'.[21] In fact, science is arguably losing some of its power at present, although its impact on how we think morally remains enormous. We have been led to view science as providing us with objective truths about the material world, and yet to believe that such knowledge has no great moral significance. Moral significance comes only when we subjectively decide which 'values' to choose in order to shape our response to the 'objective facts' provided by science.

What is more, in our technological society, we tend to view ourselves as in control. We are making and remaking the world and ourselves as we see fit, with no transcendent God or moral order. We now view ourselves as called to transcend the limits we face – including most traditional and religious forms of morality. Limits are there in order to be overcome. When such a mindset combines with the technological quest for efficiency and control, it is little surprise that the default morality for many people is a consequentialist ethic, where actions are judged right or wrong solely in terms of their outcomes or consequences. The best moral leaders are then those whose technical and bureaucratic skills make them most able to understand how to secure the consequences their followers desire. Moral leadership becomes a matter of managerial and technocratic effectiveness rather than offering and living out a way of being fully human within all the limits such a vision entails.

Those who have rejected a Christian vision of the good life often portray their morality as rational and divorced from religious commitment. In fact, as I have attempted to sketch, much contemporary understanding of what we mean by morality, and how to make moral decisions and provide moral leadership, is in fact shaped by our devotion to the idols of consumerism, individualism, and science/technique, which the chapter has identified as so important for understanding the world today.

Morality and law

A number of additional features of our moral landscape are important for any moral leader, particularly a Christian moral leader.

The first is that we find ourselves in a post-Christendom society. For many centuries the Christian church and Western society were generally viewed as coterminous, and the leaders of the church provided the spiritual and moral leadership for society as a whole. This was often enshrined in secular legislation and enforced by the coercive power of the State.

One area where this was most directly felt was in matters of sex and marriage. The moral sea change here in the last fifty years is enormous in both church and society at large. To give just one example, in 1955 Princess Margaret announced that, 'mindful of the Church's teaching', she would not marry Group Captain Peter Townsend because he was a divorcee. Now that the Church of England overwhelmingly accepts that there are circumstances in which a divorced person may be married in church during the lifetime of a former spouse, this position seems remarkable. The liberation of society from traditional sexual mores during the

1960s and after has undoubtedly had a wider knock-on effect on other areas where the church seeks to provide moral leadership. It is, of course, the reaction against such patterns of moral leadership by the church in the past that drives thinkers like Grayling, even if it is now 'faith communities' rather than the Christian church or the Church of England that are seen as a threat to the secular, liberal State.

What is perhaps more significant, though less widely recognized, is that the linkage of morality with State power and legislation is still powerful in the collective psyche of the nation. In fact, it could be argued that the modern 'liberal' State at times appears to have simply replaced the Christian church as the major determinant of society's morals. On the one hand, if a group considers something to be immoral, then, even if they consider themselves to be politically liberal or on the left, they may seek to outlaw it by legislation as seen in contemporary debates over fox hunting and smacking children. Christians, of course, often still follow a similar line of thinking, and apparently mourn the demise of Christendom. On the other hand, and fuelling this first tendency, if a way of life or form of conduct is not illegal, it can become very difficult to oppose or criticize it as immoral. After all, to call a legal action 'immoral' or, even worse, to continue to exercise traditional non-legal forms of moral censure within society questions the supremacy of individual freedom and personal choice, and apparently infringes people's legal rights. As became obvious in some of the debates surrounding the incorporation into British law of the European Convention on Human Rights, although there are great strengths in enshrining human rights in law, this is simply the legislating of mainstream morality. Once some more concrete decisions about the contents of these rights have to be made, there may well be real moral disputes. Just as with 'heretics' in Christendom, legal judgments in the future could potentially pose some interesting challenges to those, including Christians, whose way of life sits uneasily with what has become the 'moral majority'.

Morals and the media

How do moral views that might be legislated by the State get formed and gain popular support? Here, as the chapter emphasizes, the other great power is the mass media, whose divine pretensions are captured in the statement that they 'create the public world in which we all live and move and have our being'. I fear I am even more pessimistic than James about the media's impact on moral leadership. Perhaps again this is due to the influence of Ellul's work on propaganda, or to the thinking of a former London Institute lecturer, Malcolm Muggeridge, in his *Christ and the Media*.[22]

Taking each of the three senses of 'moral leader' in turn, I see the media generally in a more negative light. Rarely do they offer us appealing, positive moral leaders, and it is interesting to ask why this is the case. I think the key is found in James's crucial comment that 'there is no leadership without followership, and there can be no following with-

the god of the media remembers our sins for ever

out communication and communion'. The good is not easily transmitted by communication alone. The good requires communion and personal relationship in order to be made known; that, in part, explains why God became incarnate. But communion is precisely what the mass media cannot provide. In contrast, whenever a leader fails morally, this can be communicated, and it becomes headline news and a defining feature of that person. Furthermore, faced with true repentance and moral change, the media rarely rise above cynicism, and this again is perhaps because to discern such qualities requires real communion. In contrast to the God and Father of Jesus Christ, who liberates us from bondage to our past by the promise 'I will forgive their wickedness and will remember their sins no more' (Jer. 31:34), the god of the media remembers our sins for ever.

The media love moral leaders in the second sense of those who have a moral vision. Such vision is positively encouraged, especially when it can be communicated in imaginative rhetoric and soundbites that communicate. But then, of course, they easily turn and mock when they sense there is no substance or when reality fails to conform so easily to the leader's moral vision. Furthermore, faced with such a visionary leadership, cynicism can again triumph, as the media appear omnipresent and determined to realize here and now Jesus' words 'There is nothing concealed that will not be disclosed, or hidden that will not be made known' (Matt. 10:26). Allegedly in the public interest (which now means simply that it interests, or preferably titillates, the public), moral leaders guilty of what could be viewed as a moral lapse are brought swiftly to public judgment. One dreads to think what chance Gladstone would have had if he had faced our modern media and their inevitable interest in his nocturnal walks in the seedier parts of London!

Perhaps most damaging of all, though, is the inability of the media to provide a forum for moral leaders in the third sense of addressing moral issues. As James so vividly describes, anyone who wishes to share his or her moral vision or explain a line of moral reasoning faces insurmountable hurdles due to the very nature of the medium in which he or she is expected to communicate. There is a desire for exciting conflict and for the reduction of complex moral questions and positions to pithy soundbite summaries. A particularly striking example is the current debate about homosexuality in both church and society. In the symposium *The Way Forward?*, probably the best attempt at serious Christian moral dialogue on the subject, one author writes:

> It is a welcome and unusual opportunity for Christians from different standpoints and backgrounds to engage in measured dialogue. Often the only place that we meet is in radio

studios or in front of cameras, pitted against one another for someone else's sport and entertainment.[23]

Nothing captures this better than the infamous attempt at exorcism of Richard Kirker (leader of the Lesbian and Gay Christian Movement) outside the 1998 Lambeth Conference by Bishop Chukwuma, an event that sadly came to symbolize that meeting of Anglican church leaders and to overshadow its final statement on human sexuality.

Cautious hope

Is the context for moral leaders really so bleak? The chapter concludes by noting signs of hope, especially among young people. The two examples cited, the campaign against apartheid in South Africa and concern for the environment, are undoubtedly both important signs to which attention must be drawn. Certainly we can see here, and elsewhere, positive evidence of moral vision and determination in the contemporary world. It is good news that, despite the claims of some, total moral relativism has not swept the board, though it would be surprising, and probably practically impossible, if such a morally incoherent viewpoint were to do so.

At the risk of seeming too much of a Jeremiah, however, I am more cautious or even sceptical about investing too much hope here. It is true that there are still strong moral convictions in society, many of which Christians share or sometimes need to learn from. However, as James notes, there are often patterns of moral formation ('new indoctrination promulgated in schools') and lines of moral reasoning ('popular subscription to the utilitarian ethic') underlying these convictions that cannot be welcome to Christians because they stand in opposition to the Christian gospel. We therefore need to beware of uncritically embracing any sense of 'categorical imperatives' and 'moral duty' or heralding these as unreservedly positive signs of a necessary bulwark against post-modern relativism. If, as I've argued, moral conclusions and lines of moral reasoning are ultimately rooted in society's deeper beliefs and wider worldviews, such surface signs of moral hope need to be treated with some caution. The pattern of apparently strong moral leadership that followed the moral decadence of Weimar Germany is a frightening warning of the truth of Jesus' parable: unless the kingdom of God and the Spirit of God removes and replaces any demon, our final condition may prove worse than the first (Luke 11:19–26).

2

THE MORAL MAZE
AND THE KINGDOM

INTRODUCTION
by Charles Moore,
Editor of The Daily Telegraph

The Daily Telegraph is a paper, I like to think, above all other newspapers that takes religion seriously. We try to have an open debate; we constantly try to invite Christians, Jews, Muslims, and other faiths to take part, and we try to report on the life of the church and talk about spirituality. It seemed to us that the Millennium Dome, even before it was occupied, was a very strange way of recognizing two thousand years since the birth of Jesus, and so we did a series in our magazine about the history of Christianity, which we called *AD*. Although we didn't advertise it at all, we sold many more copies of the paper on each of the days that we produced it – a tribute to the fact that people are actually searching, and are desperately interested in all such matters. I think they feel that they do not know enough about them. And one of the functions of a newspaper should surely be to increase the information available.

Bishop James is an extremely articulate performer, and one who understands that there is no contradiction between an unambiguous Christian message and an engagement with modern society. There are many who think it has to be one or the other, and he constantly shows us by his words that it can and should be both.

In the world of newspapers, the atrocities of 11 September 2001 brought the whole idea of religion under attack, for reasons that, while I do not share, I understand. It appears that people who believe they are acting in the name of God have harder hearts than those who are not so motivated. This presents a great challenge to Christians and to people of all faiths to explain why that is precisely wrong. In order for that to be explained, we need people like Bishop James to address us on this great theme of moral leadership. In this second chapter, he discusses the moral maze and the kingdom.

The Moral Maze and the Kingdom
by James Jones

Connecting with culture

In the first chapter, I wandered through some of the avenues of the moral maze in search of today's moral leader. It was, I admit, a rather inconclusive journey, although some of the hedges were noteworthy. I want to begin to explore how the church might make connections with our culture, the moral landscape of which is changing before our eyes.

The church has before it at least two vocations: the prophetic and the pastoral. By the way she orders her life in relationships internally, and by what she proclaims publicly of God's kingdom to the world, she discharges the prophetic task of pointing up the *commandments* of God. Similarly, also by the way she orders her life in relationships internally, and by what she does in acts of justice and mercy in the wider community, she discharges the pastoral task of demonstrating the *compassion* of God.

The media, especially television, which present and interpret the world to us, not only are dogged by the binary construction referred to in the last chapter, but also are surprisingly one-dimensional in that they lack subtlety and can hold only one image at a time about any given subject. Thus the church is *either* prophetic and pointing up the commandments of God, and out of touch with the modern world, *or* pastoral and demonstrating the compassion of God, and therefore compromising its traditional values.

> *the church has before it at least two vocations: the prophetic and the pastoral*

Notwithstanding the challenges of the media, however, the church has for centuries agonized over how she relates her faith to the world. The theme is explored by the four evangelists, by St Paul, by Aquinas, by Augustine, by Luther, by Reinhold Niebuhr and by William Temple, to name a shortlist. They would all be candidates for nomination to a list of the one hundred most influential moral thinkers and leaders.

A few words about Aquinas, Augustine and Luther.

Aquinas, following Aristotle, stressed that all people are possessed of a rational ability to reflect on our human nature and to discern what is required of us to live a good life. This capacity to understand God's plan, which is built into our nature, he called natural law. Through cultivating the virtues of prudence (the ability to reason), of temperance (the ability to moderate our emotions), of courage (the ability to endure troubles) and of justice (the ability to will and to do good to others), all had the potential to aspire to a good life. This natural law is derived from

God's eternal law, which is disclosed to Christians more fully through Scripture and Christian tradition. Although Aquinas drew on Aristotle, he was able to go further than the Greek philosopher, for God has revealed his reason and his love most fully in the mercy and forgiveness of Jesus Christ. The Thomist position is that human reason in everyone is met by divine revelation through the witness of the church, which both undergirds and complements the natural law perceived by the world.

Augustine believed that all human action arises from the search for happiness. Because only God can make human beings happy, happiness can come about only through faith and obedience to God's commands. 'Our hearts are restless until they find their rest in thee.'[1] If the end is happiness, then the motivation is love. Yet there are right and wrong loves, which can be distinguished only by the quality or character of the object of the love. This provided Augustine with his definition of community: 'A people is the association of a multitude of rational beings united by a common agreement on the objects of their love.'[2] What communities love is peace.

Augustine famously contrasted two communities: the City of God constituting the elect, and the Earthly City. The former is bound for salvation and the latter for destruction. Yet whereas the Earthly City cannot benefit from the eternal destiny and peace of the City of God, the elect nevertheless are beneficiaries of the 'unequal peace' on offer by the Earthly City. The Augustinian position is that the church lives side by side with the secular State, whereby, as Oliver O'Donovan has noted, 'provisional goods may be possessed in common, without prejudice to the contrasting final destinies of two irreconcilable moral communities'.[3]

Luther also distinguished the two arenas, with his emphasis on the two realms, of creation and redemption. A Christian was at one and the same time a subject of both kingdoms. All live in the realm of creation, where the creator God's laws are imposed by the State, and all are called to live under them in civil justice and obedience. But, in the realm of redemption, the redeeming God rules all regenerate believers through the grace and Spirit of Jesus Christ, so that they respond in love and faithful obedience. Luther maintained that, whereas these two kingdoms needed always to be distinguished, they should never be separated.

Luther had a highly developed social conscience. He envisaged extensive social change through Christians being involved in transforming society, either inspired by Christ in faith-activated love or compelled by the State in law-abiding reason. Either way, the Christian, as both saint and citizen, was called to live not for self but for the benefit of others. Whereas Luther countenanced no dualistic division between the two kingdoms of creation and redemption, he was equally clear about the different roles and responsibilities therein:

> On the one side, the church should not impose its will on the civil community by usurping the power of enforcement that rightly falls within the domain of government. On the other side, the state ought not to interfere with the church's prophetic role in holding public life accountable to the sovereign law of God.

Aquinas, Augustine and Luther may not have classed themselves as moral leaders, but down the centuries they have exerted a huge influence on Christian social ethics. There are echoes in William Temple:

> There is a general knowledge of good and evil acquired through human reason and recognised by human conscience independent of Christian revelation. The Bible itself endorses this conclusion ... The image of God in man persists after the fall. The gentiles know certain moral mores in their conscience without Christian revelation ...[4]

Imposing Christian values?

But, given the delineation of the two cities, the two realms, the two kingdoms, to what extent can Christians bring to bear on others, who do not believe in God, the values of the kingdom of God? Ought they to do so? Modern social commentators who see themselves as not-Christians are often outspoken and antagonistic towards those Christians who seek to shape public policy with Christian values. One example shows where the battle-lines are drawn. The proposal that the State should reinforce both the institution of marriage and the value to social cohesion of the family by restructuring the tax and bene-fit system in favour of married couples has incurred the wrath of social commentators who resent the imposing of Christian values and the implied discrimination against those parents who do not marry.

the values explicit in the new covenant are implicit in the old

Whereas there are always those outside the church who want to retain the rigid separation of church and State, there are also siren voices within the church that go way beyond Augustine's two cities and Luther's two kingdoms, questioning the appropriateness of applying the ethics of the Christian community to the life of the wider world. Some have made a division between 'the ethics of the kingdom' and 'the ethics of creation'. But Oliver O'Donovan, in his seminal work *Resurrection and Moral Order*, disputes such a division. 'At its root there would have to be a hidden dualism which interpreted the progress of history to its completion not as a fulfilment, but as a denial of its beginnings.'[5] Can we really divide the two?

What God has revealed in Jesus Christ and through the Holy Spirit and by the New Testament is consonant with what he has revealed in creation and through the law given to Moses and by the prophets in the Old Testament. The values explicit in the new covenant are implicit in the old. There is a moral continuum between the two. Jesus did not abolish the law – neither the natural nor the Mosaic. He embodied and personified it. He radicalized it. He applied it to the heart as well as to the word and the deed. Then he dispensed mercy and forgiveness to all who fall short. There is no division between the values of creation and the values of redemption. Indeed, to imagine such a division is to suggest that creation happened once upon a time, stopped, and is now superseded by redemption. The truth – the biblical truth – is that creation has never stopped, but continues to this very moment.

Colossians 1:15–20 and Hebrews 1:1–3 see the world sustained in this very moment by the Word, through whom everything that exists has come into being. The values of creation are today's values because creation has never ceased. Thus O'Donovan continues:

> Christian moral judgments in principle address every man ... In this assertion we can find a point of agreement with the classical ethics of Plato, Aristotle and the Stoics which treated ethics as a close correlate of metaphysics. The way the universe *is*, determines how man *ought* to behave himself in it.[6]

One kingdom

I would rather approach the issue by asking the old question 'What is the kingdom of God?' Is it the church or the world? The answer Jesus gave to Nicodemus in John 3:3, 5–8 suggests that the kingdom is the church, the body of believers, whose eyes have been opened to see the kingdom and who have been born from above to enter it. Equally, the Bible makes clear that the whole earth is the Lord's and everything within it. On that reading, it seems that the kingdom is the world. I believe it is not paradoxical to conclude that the kingdom of God is at least two-dimensional, and that it is *both* the church *and* the world. Because God is Lord of lords and King of kings, not one square centimetre can be withdrawn from his sovereignty. The earth is indeed the Lord's. The rule of his kingdom extends over the face of it. The world is his kingdom, whose ethical principles, which are undivided and universal, are binding on all who inhabit the earth, regardless of culture or era.

Within the world there are those who by grace have been given insight through the Spirit to see and believe this truth that the whole world is God's kingdom. This spiritual experience is like a new birth, and brings the believer into a consciously personal relationship with the ruler of the kingdom. That relationship is marked by faith and obedience on behalf of the believer, and is expressed in the central petition of the Lord's Prayer 'your kingdom come, your will be done on earth as it is in heaven ...' (Matt. 6:10).

As that prayer is being prayed and answered, the kingship of God is being realized and actualized in a personal dimension with social consequences. The values of the kingdom are being recognized and consciously lived out. In that sense, we are seeing a manifestation of the kingship of God. Instead of seeing two kingdoms, two realms, two cities, two separate acts of God, one in creation and the other in redemption, we see one kingdom, one Lord and one act of continuous creation, in which redemption is an integral and not a separate theme and activity of God. The values of the kingdom are true and applicable to all peoples at all times. It is the calling of the church to help the world trace back from its moral and spiritual intuitions and intentions to the God who speaks in creation, in history, in the Scriptures and supremely in the person, teaching, death and resurrection of Jesus Christ – which is the method Paul seemed to be adopting with the moral and philosophical leaders in the Areopagus in Athens in Acts 17.

St Paul's understanding of the kingdom of God is found on the hinges that bind together the end of Romans 12 and the beginning of Romans 13. John Robinson, in his commentary *Wrestling with Romans*, points out that the wrath of God in 12:19 is not so much God's final judgment as the punishment meted out by the State on wrongdoers, as described by Paul in 13:1–5.[7]

What is significant in this passage is that Paul describes these State officials as 'God's deacons'. Their authority comes from God (13:1); they have been instituted and appointed by God (13:2); to resist them is to resist God and to incur his judgment; they exercise moral leadership to deter bad conduct and encourage good behaviour (13:3); and they are God's servants for our good (13:4). I know that this passage raises more questions than it settles. The one incontrovertible and influential point, however, is that these officials, who are not characterized by Christian faith and, moreover, were in the service of a corrupt empire, were seen by Paul as 'deacons of God', doing the will of God in applying the moral law to all citizens.

there is one kingdom over which God rules and within which he establishes systems of governance

There is no suggestion of two realms, two cities, two kingdoms. There is one kingdom over which God rules and within which he establishes systems of governance. That is why Christians must play their full part in paying taxes, deferring to civil authority and praying for its leaders. Clearly there will be, and have been, times when the values promulgated by the State will be at variance with the moral law of God. On those occasions Christians, and others whose conscience will not yield, will resist and take the consequences. As Peter said defiantly, 'Judge for yourselves whether it is right in God's sight to obey you rather than God. For we cannot help speaking about what we have seen and heard' (Acts 4:19–20).

Throughout the early chapters of Acts, Luke describes the

tension between the apostles and the authorities, although it is significant that the first Christians were popular with ordinary people who saw the moral quality of their lives. Yet when the authorities sought to silence the apostles, they prayed that they might 'speak the word of God with boldness' (4:29). 'Boldness' does not do justice to the meaning, for the word *parrēsia* translates more faithfully as 'freedom of speech'. Whatever the authorities, Jewish or Roman, imposed, they could not usurp their freedom of speech and their God-given calling and human right to speak about what they had 'seen and heard'.

The kingdom and the State

Within the moral law of God, freedom of speech is both a human right and a human duty. The State should ensure such freedom, both as a right and as a duty, although, as in Augustine's understanding of love, this freedom also has to be qualified by the nature, character and quality of what is spoken (for instance, by outlawing slander, libel and racism). Even though Paul himself suffered at the hands of the State, both Jewish and Roman, he nevertheless held a high view of the State within the sovereign purposes of God. Furthermore, he was neither reserved nor apologetic in claiming the benefits of the State to advance his own cause. The fact that he could say, 'Civis Romanus sum' ('I am a Roman citizen'), gave him access to the highest civil authority. He claimed the advantages of citizenship, and there is no suggestion that he saw this in contradistinction to being in Christ, or that there was any inconsistency in both calling Jesus 'Lord' and acknowledging the authority of the State and appealing to Caesar's authority – even when that State was persecuting Christians. In a sentence, there was no theological or moral objection to a Christian's acknowledging the lordship of Caesar so long as he or she confessed Jesus as Lord of all lords (cf. 1 Tim. 6:15).

It is not an exaggeration to say, with Alan Suggate, that

although the Bible 'can be critical of culture, it is certainly not counter-cultural, and it aspires to a positive relation with the State'.[8] This view of the State as integral to and not separate from the kingdom of God is essential to the debate about moral leadership in Britain today. We are at a crossroads. There are those beyond the church who want to sever all historic links between church and State, and to reduce the influence of Christian principles in public policy. My view is that, were it not for the fact that the current prime minister, Tony Blair, and several key Cabinet Ministers have their own political philosophy seriously informed by Christianity, the disentangling of these threads would be happening rapidly. What is more surprising is that voices outside the church find its walls echoing with similar dissent from those inside who call for disestablishment and for a separation of the powers of church and State.

The kingdom and the Established Church

What follows is written conscious of my position as a Church of England bishop. I believe it is relevant to finding connections between the current moral maze of our culture and a biblical vision of the kingdom of God. One of these points of connected-ness has historically been the established position of the Church of England. The argument about its future has to be conducted on two fronts – within the church and within society. As I have indicated elsewhere,[9] my support for the continued establishment of the Church of England is not because I believe that a prime minister should be involved in the appointment of bishops, although it is a curious theology that denies that God can work beyond the boundaries of the church; neither is it because I believe that bishops, along with the leaders of other denominations and faith communities, should have seats in the House of Lords (I write this as one who is not yet a member), for their presence there signals that there is an important spiritual and moral dimension to public policy. My support arises out of a theological conviction, deduced from Scripture, that in reality there is no such thing as secularism. However many people may deny God, resist his rule and disobey his commandments, God was, is and always will be, and his kingdom reigns for ever and ever.

To separate out the church from the State is a concession to an illusion that God is confined only to the affairs of the church and that the State can free itself from the sovereign rule of God. However much State office-holders may see themselves as simply public servants, Christians declare with Paul and with the eyes of faith that they are in fact 'God's deacons'. It may be uncomfortable for the church to 'hang in there' as a sign of these things – but discomfort was never a reason for a prophet to pack up his symbols, swallow his words and withdraw from the public arena.

it is a curious theology that denies that God can work beyond the boundaries of the church

My good friend the disestablishmentarian Bishop Colin Buchanan has ridiculed this position by saying that Paul's recognition of State officials as 'God's deacons' would never have led him to accept their participation in the appointment of elders in the church. But, in a sense, Paul's appeal to the emperor through declaring 'Civis Romanus sum' involved the State not only in protecting him and in exonerating him from false charges, but also in legitimizing his ministry and mission throughout the Roman Empire. The Acts of the Apostles closes with Paul living in his own rented house under the protection of the State: 'When we got to Rome, Paul was allowed to live by himself, with a soldier to guard him' (28:16). He welcomed all comers, and proclaimed the kingdom of God and taught about the Lord Jesus Christ. He was able to do this 'without hindrance' (28:31) because of the protection of the State. The closing words of Acts tell us he did so 'boldly', 'with freedom of speech', a right that he claimed from the State and a right the State safeguarded. Far from being embarrassed by this engagement with, and even indebtedness to, undemocratic and morally flawed authorities, Paul relished the opportunities that it gave him. Thus, when King Agrippa felt that he was succumbing to Paul's persuasion ('Do you think that in such a short time you can persuade me to be a Christian?'), Paul replied, 'Short time or long – I pray God that not only you but all who are listening to me today may become what I am, except for these chains' (26:28–29). I believe that establishment affords similar opportunities in our own time. (In parenthesis, Paul Avis's important book *Church, State and the Establishment* reminds us that it was the emperor Constantine who comes in for such a hard time from disestablishmentarians, who actually convened the Council of Nicea, which succinctly formulated Christian doctrine for the Western Church!)[10]

Clearly there are temptations to compromise. Against those who say that the Church of England is essentially compromised by the State's involvement in appointments, and that her prophetic voice is silenced, however, I have to record that the opposite is true. It is precisely because the State is involved in episcopal appointments that the media are for ever seeking comments, especially critical ones, from bishops! Far from the prophetic view being muted, it is magnified. Other religious leaders, such as the Chief Rabbi and the Archbishop of Armagh, do not benefit from a position in the established church; but their contributions are sought not least because of their considerable personal charisma and authority.

Pastors to the community

But the established status of the church is most important to me for what it expresses at a local level. The parish system demonstrates a particular theology of the kingdom. The vicar and the parish church serve not just the gathered congregation but the whole parish. The vicar is not chaplain to a congregation but a pastor to all who live within the parish boundaries. In Anglican ecclesiology there is a continuum between pastoral care and evangelism. A weakness arises in this view of the parish if we fail to realize that in the modern world there are also invisible parishes and networks of relationships that transcend the boundaries of geographical parishes. Yet every citizen of the planet lives in a particular place, and each place falls within the boundary of an ecclesiastical parish. A church at the centre of every parish gives expression to the writ of God's kingdom running beyond the walls of the church community up to and beyond the boundaries of the parish.

Of course, some Anglican clergy and parish churches do act as chaplains to eclectic congregations and deny that heritage. But the parish system, for all its faults, offers us a view of the kingdom in which God, through clergy and people, shows his love to the whole community. Establishment is carved out of centuries of experience of the national church set in and serving every local community, rich and poor, urban and rural, suburban, inner-city and outer-estate. Establishment is a local phenomenon whereby the church locally has proved to be a trusted servant of the neighbourhood. I admit that the experience is now patchy, but in many places it is a reality still. The role of the church in the countryside during the foot-and-mouth epidemic in 2001, the role of the church in urban regeneration and the role of church schools (which a million children attend) bear witness to the virtues of a church that is locally established and trusted.

So, as a bishop, I see myself standing in a tradition whereby I am not simply an elder within the Christian church on Merseyside, but one of the pastors to the whole community. At the enthronement, I was greeted by the Lord Mayor, who welcomed me to the city 'as a pastor and teacher and advocate of the people'. The leadership I exercise is along a continuum between church and community, which is why (for example) I accepted invitations to chair the North West Constitutional Convention, the Board of the New Deal for Community, and the Board of a new city academy. It is a theology of the kingdom that informs my conviction that the ethical values made explicit by Jesus Christ are relevant and appropriate to all people.

With Paul I pray that others may become Christians. With Paul I take the opportunities that the State offers for the advancement of the gospel. With Paul I recognize those in public service as God's deacons, whether or not they believe. I will work with them to encourage good conduct, to overturn injustice and to establish a society of justice and mercy. With Paul I recognize the reality of conflict and the inevitable clashes of values as we seek to apply God's standards to a world flawed by sin and clouded by sinister spiritual forces. With Paul I know that, in this task of proclaiming the kingdom, we need the help of every alliance possible, with those of faith and with those of no faith at all. But especially we are dependent upon 'the immeasurable greatness of the power at work in us who believe'.

> *we follow in the footsteps of Jesus, the perfect moral leader, through the moral maze of today's world*

The Spirit and the world

This dependency on the Spirit of Christ will lead us, not to retreat into an alternative city, realm or kingdom, but to engage with the world at large. As we journey through the moral maze, perhaps we might hear these words of Lesslie Newbigin:

The kingship of God, present in Jesus, concerns the whole of human life in its public as well as its private aspects. There is no basis in scripture for the withdrawal of the public aspect of human life from that obedience which the disciple owes to the Lord. The question, therefore, is not: 'What grounds can be shown for Christian involvement in public life?' It is: 'What grounds can be shown for the proposal to withdraw from the rule of Christ the public aspects of our human living?' The answer is: 'None.'[11]

Then, as we follow in the footsteps of Jesus, the perfect moral leader, through the moral maze of today's world, we should pray that we too may have this manifesto on our hearts:

'The Spirit of the Lord is on me,
    because he has anointed me
    to preach good news to the poor.
He has sent me to proclaim freedom for the prisoners
    and recovery of sight for the blind,
to release the oppressed,
    to proclaim the year of the Lord's favour.'

(Luke 4:18–19)

Here is a manifesto of moral and spiritual leadership: the values of the kingdom spoken in space and time in a synagogue in Nazareth for all the world. And when he told them that these values, like God's love, were for all the world, even and especially for those they hated, they blocked their ears, and, full of rage, tried to throw him off the cliff. Such is the courage required by the moral leader who applies the values of the kingdom to the kingdom of God.

RESPONSE
by Andrew Goddard

In my experience, the best theological conversations take place
when I am in neither total agreement nor fundamental disagreement with someone, and feel able to be open and honest about
where I differ. It enables me to think through my position more
clearly and to think through why the differences are present and
how important they are. I want to begin my response to chapter 2
by highlighting the many significant areas where we are in
agreement. For much of my response, however, I want to explore
why, despite these important and fundamental points in common,
I would develop an alternative understanding of the relationship
between church, society and the State, and hence a different
assessment of establishment and moral leadership.

Gospel and culture

The chapter's stated aim is clear and crucial, but one that, for much of the last century, evangelicals somehow failed to take seriously: to explore how the church might make connections with our culture. It identifies and explores three key areas central in my own approach to these questions.

First and foremost, it is vital to recognize that the gospel we have received and are called to proclaim is public truth, good news for this world, that relates to the whole of life.

For a variety of reasons many Christians, including, tragically, some evangelical Christians who emphasize the centrality of the gospel, have reduced the gospel in a narrow and unbiblical way. The gospel message easily becomes only an offer of other-worldly salvation for individual souls, a passport to heaven for when we die. This universal and transcultural gospel, focused exclusively on Christ's death for our sins, is then addressed to individuals who must decide whether or not to accept it personally. Such an understanding can clearly claim biblical support for many of its central themes, and that is partly why it is so persuasive. Perhaps, however, its attraction also lies in its parallels with the three main idols we identified earlier. It simplifies and distorts Scripture in order to offer an attractive product the church can sell for consumers in the religious marketplace. It is individualistic, exalting individual choice and fulfilment. It offers a quasi-scientific account of how the spiritual world and divine redemption work. While such resonances with our culture may be a sign of a wise, pragmatic evangelistic strategy, few who advocate this 'gospel' present it in such terms of a faithful and effective contextualization. In fact, I fear that for all its talk about sin and the need for repentance and salvation, it represents a subtle conformity to culture, which leaves little or no basis in the gospel for speaking about ethics and moral leadership or connecting with culture as a whole.

In contrast, this chapter refocuses our attention on the heart of Jesus' own message in the proclamation of the kingdom of God and the prophetic and pastoral vocation this gospel gives to the church. Following Christ's death, resurrection and ascension, the apostolic church gave form to this kingdom proclamation in the central, foundational Christian confession that 'Jesus is Lord' (Rom. 10:9; 1 Cor. 12:3). The holistic biblical gospel is therefore that the reign of God and the redemption of God's world have been established by God himself in the life, death and resurrection of Jesus Christ. This one whom we rejected and crucified has defeated sin, death and all the rebellious powers we humans worship and serve, and he is now exalted as Lord of all. When the Christian church places this biblical gospel at the centre of its life, all sorts of other pieces fall into place. The church is then enabled to be the church in and for the world, with a gospel that can connect – though never easily or comfortably – with every person and culture.

One of my favourite summaries of how such a gospel connects is found in the Barmen Declaration, written by the great Swiss theologian Karl Barth in 1934, which shaped Christian opposition to the Nazi regime. It includes the following ringing declarations in its opening paragraphs:

> Jesus Christ, as he is attested to us in Holy Scripture, is the one Word of God which we have to hear, and which we have to trust and obey in life and in death ... As Jesus Christ is God's comforting pronouncement of the forgiveness of all our sins, so, and with equal seriousness, he is also God's vigorous announcement of his claim upon our whole life. Through him there comes to us joyful liberation from the godless ties of this world for free, grateful service to his creatures. We reject the false doctrine that there could be areas of our life in which we would belong not to Jesus Christ but to other lords ... [12]

Another favourite summary is much more of a memorable soundbite. It comes from the great nineteenth-century Dutch

Reformed thinker and politician Abraham Kuyper, at the opening of the Free University in Amsterdam:

> There is not a single inch of the whole terrain of our human existence over which Christ ... does not proclaim, 'Mine!' [13]

As the chapter's wonderful closing passage from Lesslie Newbigin illustrates, such a perspective means that the gospel is what drives the church into the world because the gospel is public truth. It not only offers eternal hope to each person, but it shapes how we are called to live here and now (Phil. 1:27), and so connects to and challenges every human culture.

the gospel is what drives the church into the world

Secondly, this gospel is therefore one in which God's work of salvation is positively related to God's work of creation. It is good news of the redemption *of* creation, not good news of our individual redemption *from* creation. As the chapter points out, passages such as Colossians 1:15–20 make this continuity between creation and redemption crystal clear. It is based on the person and work of Jesus Christ, the Word of God, who has not only redeemed the world, but is the one by whom, and through whom, and for whom, all things were made. To say anything else is to get close to the gnostic heresies the early church opposed because they denied the goodness of God's creation and because their vision of redemption involved escape from the body and matter.

In relation to ethics and the moral leader, this means, of course, that sharp divisions between 'the ethics of the kingdom' and 'the ethics of creation' are fundamentally flawed, as James explains by reference to Oliver O'Donovan. At the risk, however, of letting one of my concerns intrude when I am meant to be highlighting where we agree, it is important to note that O'Donovan's critique is of 'a kingdom ethics which was set up *in opposition* to creation'.[14] We need to beware, however, of allowing no difference between the two. Jesus' practice and teaching concerning celibacy demonstrate that the 'fulfilment' of creation may not be a simple reiteration of created order. There is also an element of newness in the kingdom he brings that encourages and enables new forms of life not given in creation. Furthermore, the fallen nature of the world means that, as we hear Christ's call to follow him and to take up our cross, faithfulness to God might now indicate that the ethics of the kingdom requires a self-denial and a self-sacrifice that were never God's good intention in creation.

Thirdly, the chapter highlights that, in order to explore how the church connects with culture, we need to focus on the relationship of Christian faith and the kingdom of God to the fallen world in which we live. One important subset of this is the relationship with political authority in the world. Since the church has indeed agonized for centuries over this question, it is perhaps no surprise that, while agreeing that this is centre stage, it is at this point that I can perhaps begin to try to explain where I look at things differently from the way set out in this chapter.

One reign, two ages

At the heart of this debate is the issue of how best to hold together both the one, universal reign of God and the strong strand of a duality that runs through both Scripture and, as discussed in relation to Augustine and Luther, the mainstream Christian tradition, with its talk of two cities or two kingdoms. The chapter focuses this on asking whether the kingdom of God is the church or the world, and concludes that 'the kingdom of God is at least two-dimensional, and that it is both the church and the world'. It then pursues this to argue that 'there is no suggestion of two realms, two cities, two kingdoms. There is one kingdom ... ' As I have struggled to work out why I can agree with so much of what is said in this chapter, and yet also disagree strongly with James's views on the State and establishment, I think the root of the problem lies here.

My worry is that this way of thinking appears to have effectively removed the elements of duality that I think are essential for a Christian understanding of the church and its connection to culture. That duality is not, I want to stress, the sort of dualism that sometimes arises among Christians and divides heaven and earth, the material and the spiritual, the body and the soul into opposing camps. It is rather a duality that arises from the existence of sin in the world and the manner of God's dealing with it in Christ.

*'the age to come'
has already
broken into
the present*

This duality arises from the classic Jewish belief in the 'two ages'. There is 'this present evil age' (Gal. 1:4), and the hoped-for 'age to come'. These two ages are explicitly mentioned together in such New Testament passages as Matthew 12:32; Mark 10:30; Luke 18:30 and Ephesians 1:21, and, even when the terms are not present, the idea is central to early Christian faith: Paul's flesh/Spirit and Adam/Christ contrasts and John's language of 'the world' come out of this understanding. What is central in the first Christian communities, and distinguishes them from the wider Jewish belief system, is their belief that 'the age to come' has already broken into the present in Christ and in the gift of his Spirit to those who are in Christ. The 'age to come' is no longer all in the future and only to be looked forward to, but neither has it yet arrived in all its fullness. It is both 'now' and also 'not yet', and so there is a real and painful tension and conflict between these two ages. There is, of course, only one true kingdom – the kingdom of God – and in Christ this kingdom, as Barth and Kuyper remind us, claims all of human life. But there are also still 'the kingdoms of the world' (Matt. 4:8; Luke 4:5) and 'the rulers of this age' (1 Cor. 2:6, 8). We have not yet reached the day when 'The kingdom of the world has become the kingdom of our Lord and of his Christ' (Rev. 11:15).

It is this way of looking at human history that explains Jesus' statement 'My kingdom is not of this world' (John 18:36). This has often been misunderstood in a dualistic fashion, as if the world in the sense of God's material creation is not the place Christ seeks to rule: his concern is really heaven. Yet Christ's rule, the kingdom of God, is not divorced from this world – that is why, as the chapter reminds us, he taught us to pray, 'Your kingdom come, your will be done on earth as it is in heaven' (Matt. 6:10). In his trial scene before the representative of Roman power, Jesus sharply contrasts the character and nature of his own rule with that of worldly rulers, as represented by Pilate. He goes on to emphasize that the decisive difference is that, if his kingdom were of this world, 'my servants would fight to prevent my arrest' (John 18:36), whereas his rule is not established by force but in another manner by God (cf. 2 Cor. 10:3–4 for how this is reworked in the apostolic mission).

This duality is, however, not simply an eschatological one between the present age and the future, final age to come. Because of the coming of Christ, there is, in addition, the historical duality of 'now' and 'not yet'. It is this duality, derived from the theology of an overlap of the two ages, that is lived out here and now, and so is a pressing issue in thinking about how the church connects with wider society, culture and the state.

The kingdom, the church and the world

James asks, 'What is the kingdom of God? Is it the church or the world?' His reply is 'Both.' If I were forced to answer that question, I would want instead to say, 'Neither,' but my real problem is more with the question than with the answer.

The language of the kingdom of God is first and foremost to be understood as referring to God, and not to part of God's creation, whether the church or the world. It speaks of God ruling or reigning, rather than of a particular location or community within time and space, as in 'United Kingdom'. As the New Testament scholar R. T. France has written:

> There can be no one place, time, event or community which is 'the kingdom of God', any more than 'the will of God' can be tied down to any specific situation or event. 'The kingdom of God' is God in saving action, God taking control in his world, or, to use our title, 'divine government'.[15]

From this perspective on the kingdom, the relationship between church and world begins to look significantly different. In a popular summary of the apostle John's teaching, the church is to be in the world but not of the world. The church is in the world in order to bear witness to a different way of life, a way of life 'not of this world'. That way of life is shaped by God's work, word and call on our lives. It is, as already seen, a way of life that connects with the whole of life and is offered to the whole world, for God seeks for us to acknowledge in our lives his wise rule over all he has made. The world at present, however, does not recognize or welcome this rule. This is clear from the way it responded to Jesus and his first disciples: 'I have given them your word and the world has hated them, for they are not of the world any more than I am of the world' (John 17:14). This is understood by Paul as the blinding of people's minds by what he calls 'the god of this age' (2 Cor. 4:4).

It is true that the church regularly fails in its calling to be in the world but not of it. It often falls captive to the powers of the world and ceases to provide a foretaste of the age to come in the present age. This is a serious error, and one that prophetic moral leaders in the church need to warn against.[16] God is, however, thankfully not limited to the church in his work in his world. There are therefore also occasions when it is necessary to say that the rule of God has been at least as evident within the world *outside* the official boundaries of the church. France again writes, 'As God the king exercises his authority in his world, and people respond to it, there the "kingdom of God" will be experienced in many ways.'[17] I do not see it as a sign that the kingdom of God is in some important sense both the church and the world. It is rather a sign that God's grace and his kingly rule are not overcome by the church's sin and failure to be what she is meant to be – the church of God in the world, sanctified in Christ Jesus, and called to be holy (cf. 1 Cor. 1:2).

This different understanding of the kingdom of God, and hence of the place and nature of the division between the church and the world, leads to concerns in three areas crucial for our thinking about moral leadership and the church's relationship to society and culture today.

First, after emphasizing 'one kingdom, one Lord', James set out the calling of the church in the following terms:

> The values of the kingdom are true and applicable to all peoples at all times. It is the calling of the church to help the world trace back from its moral and spiritual intuitions and intentions to the God who speaks in creation, in history, in the Scriptures and supremely in the person, teaching, death and resurrection of Jesus Christ.

It seems to me that this statement translates the sense of 'the kingdom' as God at work, establishing his rule, into the popular but, to my mind, also often unhelpful moral language of 'values'. These values are then seen to be in some sense represented, however dimly, in the world's own 'moral and spiritual intuitions'. The church is called to take these intuitions rather than the gospel of God's rule and Christ's lordship as its starting point in a mission that assists the world by tracing them back to God.

Later in the chapter we read that 'in this task of proclaiming the kingdom, we need the help of every alliance possible, with those of faith and with those of no faith at all'. While I am happy for Christians to work with others who share some of their vision of society's common good, I would not express such collaboration in terms of 'proclaiming the kingdom', or speak of the church's *need* to find worldly allies in the task of making known God's good news in word and deed.

Such a statement seems to me to diminish the serious effect of sin on humanity and the continued strength of the principalities and powers in human society. I struggle to see how this account of the church's calling fits with the radical (and, in an important sense, counter-cultural) message that burst upon Israel at the start of Jesus' ministry: 'Repent, for the kingdom of heaven is near' (Matt. 3:2; cf. Mark 1:15). Although not without its weaknesses, I find the description of the church's calling provided by Stanley Hauerwas much closer to the gospel message:

> The first social task of the church – the people capable of remembering and telling the story of God we find in Jesus – is to be the church and thus help the world understand itself as world. That world, to be sure, is God's world, God's good creation, which is all the more distorted by sin because it is still bounded by God's goodness. For the church to be the church, therefore, is not anti-world, but rather an attempt to show what the world is meant to be as God's good creation.[18]

Establishment and prophetic critque

The second sphere in which I view things significantly differently is in the assessment the church should have of political authority in the world and hence, in modern terms, of leadership (including moral leadership) on the part of the State. This obviously derives in part from our differences over the language of the kingdom of God, but also from a different interpretation of the biblical witness concerning political power.

James refers to Luther's doctrine of the two kingdoms or governments. The exact nature of Luther's own understanding and how it developed over time is highly contentious, not least because of the way he was read (better, misread) by later German Lutherans, with disastrous consequences for the church's witness in the face of Nazism's rise. At its heart, however, is a further duality, which is not that between the present age and the age to come, or between the kingdom of darkness and the kingdom of Christ (Col. 1:13). Luther also taught that there are two ways in which God rules his creation – law and gospel. These he often depicted as the right hand and left hand of divine government. In relation to the State and secular law and punishment, this leads, as in this chapter, to a strong emphasis on Romans 13 and to the argument that the political authority is to be recognized and welcomed as God's servant exercising his wrath. Clearly that text is important, but I think it can be read properly only in the light of the whole of Scripture, and that when this is done it leads to a different emphasis from that presented in this chapter, and so to a quite different understanding of church establishment.

When I look at how God engages the world of politics in Scripture, I see two strands running through both the Old and the New Testament and in constant dialogue with each other.[19] These could be described as the 'establishment' strand and the 'non-conformist' or 'critical' strand. The former (classically represented by Rom. 13) relates to the role and responsibilities of ruling powers and existing political authorities. The latter represents a dissenting critique of established political power. Thus, in the Pentateuch, we see the 'critical' perspective evident in the foundational event of the exodus from Egypt. Alongside this, however, is the giving of the law to the liberated people of God in order to structure and guide their common life. Both the liberation from State oppression in Egypt and the commands of God at Sinai need to be held together in any theological ethic, and particularly in Christian political thinking.

Once Israel was settled in the Promised Land, there were struggles over the structure of political power. These resulted in the establishment of the monarchy, although not without a sense that this was a disobedient and potentially dangerous development in Israel's relationship with God (Judg. 9; 1 Sam. 8 – 12; Deut. 17:14–20). There was, nevertheless, a clear sense that God would provide and work through monarchs who acted wisely and obeyed his call to seek and establish justice among his people. It is here that we find the classic Old Testament 'establishment' texts, such as the royal psalms (Pss. 72; 89; 101; 110) and the sayings of the king in Proverbs 31, which provide so much wisdom for those who seek to be moral leaders in the different senses discussed earlier.

we see what true kingship is, as Jesus proclaims and enacts the rule of God on earth

Clearly, however, Israel's history demonstrates that her rulers all fell short of this divine political calling, and so we find the hope developing of a true ruler, described, for example, in the familiar text of Isaiah 9:1–7. We also discover that the 'critical' strand has not disappeared, as, through numerous prophets, God speaks directly to rulers (e.g. through Nathan in 2 Sam. 11 – 12) and challenges rulers and ruled within Israel, not least about injustice and oppression (Amos, Micah, etc.).

Much more could be said about the politics of the Old Testament (e.g. the significance of figures such as Joseph, Esther and Daniel, who served in a pagan context), but, for Christians, at the centre of revelation is Jesus Christ. In God's becoming human we see the two strands in Old Testament Israel coming together to meet as God re-establishes his rule over his people. We see what true kingship is, as Jesus proclaims and enacts the rule of God on earth in his own ministry, summed up in the Nazareth manifesto of Luke 4, with which the chapter ends. But, of course, that is only one side of the story. The other side is Jesus the prophet, who, from the moment of his birth (according to Matthew) challenged the political rulers. Herod he called 'that fox' (Luke 13:32), and his famous response to the question about paying tribute (Mark 12:13–17) – another frequently misunderstood saying – left his scheming opponents amazed because of its ambiguity. It should therefore be no great surprise that the State system sought to eliminate him and his message about another king, who was establishing his rule in Caesar's realm. In the light of this gospel witness, I would be interested to learn how James would unpack his statement that 'the State, as integral to and not separate from the kingdom of God, is essential to the debate about moral leadership in Britain today'.

The chapter's argument leading to this conclusion is focused on Romans 13 and a reading of Paul's personal relationship with the State. Obviously, Paul here (as in the 'establishment' strand in the Old Testament) speaks highly of those through whom God is at work in their exercise of public judgment. But this is not the only image of the State in the apostolic witness. Elsewhere, the 'critical' strand reappears, most notably in the book of Revelation and its image of the Beast in Revelation 13. Certainly the New Testament is clear that the continued existence of political power, even if used by God in his providential and preserving rule, is a sign that God's kingdom is not yet fully here and that we still look forward eagerly to the time when Christ 'hands over the kingdom to God the Father after he has destroyed all dominion, authority and power' (1 Cor. 15:24). In short, I personally find this chapter's reading of Scripture too focused on one side of what I believe to be a much more dialectical relationship.

This in turn leads me, thirdly, to the question of establishment. I am one of the 'surprising' voices inside the church calling 'for dis-establishment and a separation of the powers of church and State'.

As often in debates, a problem here is definitions. Like James, I value the parish system and the fact that the Church of England seeks to serve the whole of England. As the examples from his own ministry show, these features can indeed remind us of the universal scope of God's purposes and provide an institutional impetus towards mission. They are not, however, the heart of what it is to be an established religion, for 'an established religion is subject to state control as regards doctrine, government, and discipline, but an unestablished religion is not'.[20]

The historic theological rationale for the Church of England's establishment is clear. It is evident in the 1604 canons (which remained in force until 1969), where, right at the beginning, we are told:

> Whosoever shall hereafter affirm that the king's majesty hath not the same authority in causes ecclesiastical that the godly kings had amongst the Jews and Christian emperors of the primitive church ... let him be excommunicated *ipso facto* and not restored, but only by the archbishop, after his repentance, and public revocation of those his wicked errors.[21]

As someone who grew up in the Church of Scotland, I know that the features of the Church of England both James and I wish to maintain and which are often understood as part of 'establishment' do not require establishment in this proper legal sense. Diarmaid MacCulloch's recent biography of Thomas Cranmer reveals, in a similar vein, that Cranmer believed that the apostolic church was deficient because it lacked Christian rulers to govern it.[22]

Given how little support such a theology would gain today, it is unsurprising that over recent decades the nature of establishment has been changed in various ways. Nevertheless, a number of significant (and to my mind indefensible) aspects of establishment remain, notably in the manner of appointing bishops and the related granting of episcopal presence in the House of Lords. James avoids a definitive statement on whether he defends these practices, and yet his comments on them intrigue me. My theology does not deny 'that God can work beyond the boundaries of the church', but I fail to see how such a perception of disestablishmentarian views connects to debates about Crown appointments. In the first place, the fact that God *can* work in a particular way does not defend church acceptance of a practice. The fact that God used Babylon to enact his judgment on Israel does not mean it would have been right for prophets to seek their authorization from Nebuchadnezzar. But the present system does not in any case claim to require God to work outside the church. It gives the power of appointment to one particular member of the church – the monarch (in reality now the prime minister) – on the basis of that individual's political status and power.

a system of church establishment is a serious handicap and not a strength

When I was studying British politics, my tutor, David Butler, always used to talk about 'the law of anticipated reactions' as crucial in assessing the real, hidden power of political institutions. The very existence of parliamentary Select Committees, in other words, acts as a check on what Government departments might think of doing, just in case they come under scrutiny. I fear that establishment builds the church into the same system of political power, and so that law works also in the church and shapes the church's psychology and her political voice, often unsubconsciously. As a result, there is great risk in any church leader acting like Micaiah, of whom the State power says, 'I hate him, because he never prophesies anything good about me, but always bad' (1 Kgs. 22:8). There will still be bold and powerfully prophetic moral leaders among the bishops, such as George Bell during the Second World War. It is, however, surely more significant that he was the only Anglican bishop in the Lords to condemn our indiscriminate blanket bombings, and that, as a result, any prospect of promotion to Canterbury was removed. One can see why the Principal of Ridley Hall, when visiting Germany in 1933, found it embarrassing that challenges concerning the religious independence of the Hitlerized church (opposed by Barth's Barmen Declaration, noted earlier) were met with 'Who appoints *your* bishops?' The very fact that, in debates about senior church appointments, it can still be *suggested* that candidates are handicapped because their pattern of moral leadership is unwelcome to those with political power is, I believe, a sign that the current establishment of the church is nothing short of scandalous, and that it seriously compromises moral leadership in our nation.

Even were I to be more convinced by the understanding of the State's positive role in God's kingdom set out in the chapter, the historic reality of State abuse of its power would make me cautious about tying a vision of Christian moral leadership too closely to the established nature of the church. My own reading finds a dialectic within the biblical witness, in which God works both through the established political authorities and through critical and prophetic voices distinct from political power. Even if this has only a grain of truth, a system of church establishment is a serious handicap and not a strength, because it upsets this dialectic by tying, indeed subjecting, the church too closely to political power. By allowing the political power such control within the church of Christ, establishment creates an institutional bias that tends against the emergence of church leaders who, when and where necessary, will follow the example of Christ and confront the kingdoms of this world with the challenge of the topsy-turvy kingdom of God.

3

THE MORAL BRIDGE OVER TROUBLED WATERS

INTRODUCTION
by Lord Griffiths of Fforrestfach, Vice-chairman of Goldman Sachs International

Throughout his life, James has placed great emphasis on evangelism, on mission, and on proclaiming the good news. At present he is Chairman of the Church of England Board of Mission. Apart from evangelism one of his major concerns has been to integrate faith with the realities of life in the world. He has taken a leadership role in regional development in the North West and has been instrumental in setting up a City academy with a Christian foundation in Liverpool.

This third chapter wrestles with the question of how we relate moral leadership to a pluralist world. Recently I was asked to address a conference at the University of Leiden in Holland, which was attended by 250 students from Dutch universities and 250 people in leadership positions in Dutch society. They asked the speakers to base our lectures on a poem that the students had written, entitled 'The world of I'. It was about personal autonomy, the dominance of work, and the need to put 'me' first. It made a great impact on me in making me realize how extraordinarily secular the world has become in a few decades. To try to introduce the Christian faith into such an environment and to maintain that there is such a thing as truth was embarrassing. I spent twenty years of my life in the university world and taught at the London School of Economics. I felt I knew what secularism was about, but I have to confess I had not grasped the full extent of the inroads it has made. The subject of this chapter is therefore vitally important.

The Moral Bridge
Over Troubled Waters
by James Jones

Moral law and moral language

Joseph Fletcher, in his biography of William Temple, argues, 'Temple's point was that the reality is there whether men perceive it or not, and in the same way values are there whether men appreciate them or not.' He quotes a ditty doing the rounds in Oxford at the time:

> There was a young man who said, 'God
> Must think it exceedingly odd
>   If he finds that this tree
>   Continues to be
> When there's no one about in the Quad.'

To which the reply was:

> Dear Sir, Your astonishment's odd
> *I* am always about in the Quad.
>> And that's why the tree
>> Will continue to be,
> since observed by Yours faithfully, God.

Just as two and two always make four, even though there may not be a mind to perceive it, so the moral law exists regardless of whether or not it is seen or even obeyed. The moral law belongs to the character of God. It is contingent on his existence, not ours, although we are beneficiaries.

It is intuited through the sentiments, reason, language and actions of human beings. From an early age children begin to handle moral categories. For example, a child as young as two, seeing her sister with more Smarties than she has, might well swipe both them and her sister, with the declaration 'Not fair!' Some will argue that these are early signs of moral conditioning and social determinism. But the fact is that here is a moral awareness – expressed in moral language, categories and actions.

Let us leave aside for a moment the source or origin of the moral intuition or what I have described elsewhere as the moral instinct.[1] Let us simply take at face value that all people, from the youngest to the oldest, use moral language and categories, and that they do so in a not entirely meaningless way. In other words, they are not just expressing personal or social preference, psychologically or sociologically conditioned, but they do in some sense believe that the words carry the weight, to some degree or another, of moral obligation.

Moral language is also a fact of public discourse. The words 'good', 'better', 'bad', 'worse', pepper conversations and debates. Political manifestos and social commentary trade in these values all the time. Nevertheless, into the language creep other words that show a society whose leaders are increasingly coy about such absolute moral categories as good and bad. Thus 'right' and 'wrong' give way to words such as 'appropriate' and 'inappropriate'. Although I understand the reticence of politicians to talk explicitly of morality, for fear of being outed as hypocrites who do not practice what they preach, I cannot agree with those who say that politics must be divorced from morality. How can you campaign for a better society without some definition of what is good or bad? Morality and politics belong together like fire and heat. Politics without morality is sheer pragmatism; morality without politics is unrealistic idealism.

But those wishing to sail their ship on the high seas of moral discourse will find that the waters have become exceedingly choppy, roughed up by the three 'M's – the media, the market, and multiculturalism.

I cannot agree with those who say that politics must be divorced from morality

The media give instant and equal access to every contrary view, so that, should someone advance a moral position on abortion, sexuality, globalization, the environment, cloning or genetic modification, the media will scour every corner to find the opposing opinion, preferably expressed in the most extreme terms possible. This brings immoderate views into the mainstream of public debate, and gives them as much oxygen as moderate views, in the name of a specious principle called 'balance'.

The market has emerged as the latest moral arbiter. If an idea sells, it's cool and right. In a culture where choice and the right to choose are elevated to a moral principle, whatever the individual chooses in the marketplace is good and right and not to be denied, so long as it does not harm anyone else, at least visibly and in the short term.

Multiculturalism rightly recognizes that there is a variety of sub-cultures, each with its own cherished traditions and beliefs. Even though most of the faith communities agree on many fundamental social and moral issues, the constant emphasizing of the principle of diversity feels like someone tugging and pulling the moral carpet from beneath our feet, undermining the appeal to an objective and coherent moral law. The very multiplicity of belief systems is used by the advocates of relativism as a signal of the lack of any absolute truth.

Moral ground

One reaction to all of this is to give up in despair, to retreat, shaking the dust off our feet, into our fortified City of God, to pull up the drawbridge and wait for the Day of Judgment. Another reaction is to recognize the battle-lines and, from a secure position, conduct occasional sorties into the big, bad world to capture and rescue the occasional soul and bring it into the fold. These reactions may be seen on the pages of church history and in the church today. But I want to suggest another way, which is consistent with Paul, Aquinas and Temple (I will come to Jesus in my final chapter). I hope Augustine and Luther might also approve, even though our cultural context is very different.

I want to propose that, in spite of all the postmodernist critique, there might yet be some common moral ground on which we might all stand – Christian, theist, those of other faiths, atheist, humanist and agnostic; and that, standing on this ground in solidarity with our society, we might with integrity be able to point to a hinterland, the vision of which might be seen through the eyes of faith. What I propose to identify is a latter-day Athenian altar. Paul identified an altar in Athens as a bridge between what the philosophers believed and what he had been destined to proclaim (see Acts 17:16–34). He recognized in them a spiritual instinct. Stoic and Epicurean philosophers made the connection between the metaphysical and the moral. Paul, although distressed by all the idols in the city (verse 16), pointed constructively to the altar with the inscription 'TO AN UNKNOWN GOD' (verse 23). He walked on to this bridge, identifying with their world, in the hope that they too would walk on to the bridge and identify with his: 'What you worship as something unknown I am going to proclaim to you' (verse 23). He entered into their world further by quoting from their poets, and took a radical step of citing an inscription to Zeus 'We are his offspring', and applying it to the God of Abraham and Jesus (verse 28). I have heard some people dispute the relevance of this passage to contemporary mission, because some of Paul's hearers scoffed. Yet Dionysius and Damaris, with others, became believers. As Chair of the Board of Mission of the Church of England, I would settle for that level of response!

The significance lies in Paul's method of finding common ground in their aspirations, their symbols and their literature. This is the model I want to follow adventurously.

Notwithstanding the confusion of moral language and moral categories in our modern moral maze, the media are for ever searching for people to express their views in the strongest moral language and categories. This is a moral climate in which we live and move and have our being, even though the triumph of the individual over the community is summed up by that Old Testament adage 'Everyone did as he saw fit' (Judg. 21:25). Even so, there is a moral awareness, especially (I want to emphasize), among young people.

Moral awe

My proposal is that the time has now come when we should call for a recovery of moral awe. Most are agreed that we have reached a watershed in our planet's history. The blind faith in science has been seriously undermined by the spectre of human cloning, genetically modified foods, the destruction of the ozone layer, global warming and discarded human organs from medical research. The sacrifice of the planet on the altar of consumerism may briefly placate the gods of multinational companies, but is leaving the worshippers and consumers increasingly fearful and alienated. The autonomy of the individual may yet be deeply embedded in our culture, but even now there are signs that an expression of belonging and mutual responsibility are personally healthier and socially more constructive; moreover, in such a climate the well-being of the individual is more secure.

As we face some of the major moral dilemmas in areas such as the environment, biotechnology and social relationships, our society *needs* a recovery of moral awe. I am not suggesting that there is a set of pat moral answers that can be applied in a 'one size fits all' manner to every ethical dilemma, not least because, as the technology develops at such a speed, we are constantly finding ourselves in new situations for which previously received moral categories are now inappropriate. I am calling for a new common moral attitude, around which we can, as a society, unite – so that the scientist in the laboratory, the politician writing a manifesto, the civil servant drafting legislation, the community member planning a regeneration scheme, the young person thinking about his or her future, the parent about to reward or discipline a child, the doctor enabling a patient to make a difficult decision, the trade unionist defending a member, the manager deciding about the future of the company, and the marketing director assessing the market for a product will all contemplate the task with moral awe.

In particular, this awe will be characterized by four hallmarks. First, all our actions spring from and shape our characters. Secondly, all our actions have consequences, individually and socially. Thirdly, all our actions will be judged by future generations. Fourthly, we are all responsible for our actions to whatever or whoever is the source of our moral intuition.

I believe that this sense of moral awe can be owned by people of all faiths and no faith. From a Christian point of view, it provides a moral bridge over the troubled waters and choppy seas of social change, enabling us to enter into dialogue with those beyond the boundary of Christian faith. It is also consonant with the revelation in Jesus Christ. Again, as Alan Suggate has written in his biography of William Temple:

> Since morality is fundamentally objective and moral discourse rational, then natural morality can form a bridge between Christian and non-Christian, enabling them to communicate, find common ground and co-operate. This is vital in an increasingly pluralistic world.[2]

One response to this plea for the recovery of moral awe might be to ask, 'So what?' Obviously, no-one hell-bent on a path of sheer selfishness would be arrested by such an appeal. Such people have to be restrained by external sanctions, should society deem their behaviour destructive. Yet the recovery of moral awe *is* relevant, for it speaks into a world as it already is, dominated by the media, the market and multiculturalism. It begins with how things are, and provides those of us who use moral language and categories with a framework for the moral debate and a common *modus operandi* as we face and make life-changing decisions. In a world dominated by the media and their relentless pressure to polarize every issue into extremes, it provides a quadrilateral within which to conduct the ethical debate. In a world dominated by the market and its elevation of the individual over the community, it locates the individual's choice within the indisputable dimensions of personal and social consequence. In a world of multiculturalism, it recognizes the common ground that exists between faith and no faith, and that diversity of religion need not detract from a belief in a moral law that is external, objective and binding on all.

In particular, the hallmarks of moral awe do not just give to those in leadership within our society a set of principles to steer them in their decision-making, but they actually encourage a more radical attitude in the decision-making process. They have the potential to produce in them the virtue of humility. In his summary of the Reith Lectures 2000, Prince Charles called for this attitude to characterize our approach to the world:

> Faced with such unknowns it is hard not to feel a sense of humility, wonder and awe about our place in the natural order. And to feel this at all stems from that inner heartfelt reason which sometimes despite ourselves is telling us that we are intimately bound up in the mysteries of life and that we don't have all the answers.[3]

In every decision we should be aware of our own personal autonomy and how the outcome will continue to shape our character; we need to realize that every cause has an effect and every action a consequence, however small, not just personally but socially; we do well to recognize that the future will judge our present as surely as we judge the past; and whatever or whoever is the source of our moral intuition will be the final arbiter and the one to which or to whom we are ultimately responsible.

Moral debate

All of this is extremely consonant with Christianity and provides a bridge over which two-way traffic can cross. It enables the Christian to stand on common ground with the world and to bear witness there to the fuller revelation of the mind and heart of God in Jesus Christ. It is on this same bridge that we can encounter people of other faiths in exactly the way that Paul did in Athens. The issue of interfaith relations has sometimes been reduced to the polarization of dialogue versus proclamation. I want to suggest a third way, exemplified by Paul, namely proclamation in the context of dialogue. In other words, as we listen to one another with mutual respect, so we reserve the right to testify to each other of those things we hold dear in our religious experience.

But dialogue, and the ethical debate in which moral leadership is immersed, means listening and learning as well as telling and teaching. It is vital to all relationships if they are to move beyond the superficial. The church and the moral leaders need to be seen and heard listening to the world. This is difficult to do, for the media, with their inherent tendency to polarize and to dramatize, want people to pontificate from extreme corners of the ring. (How things change! To 'pontificate' originally meant 'to bridge-build', but has come to mean 'to shout stridently, stranded on one side of the argument'.) That listening has taken place in recent church history. For example, new attitudes to women and to the environment did not form first within the church, except for a few rare exceptions. The lead on these moral issues came from beyond the barriers of the formal church. To view this negatively, one could say that this was yet another example of the church hide-bound by tradition and closed off to the prophetic voice of the Spirit. To see it positively,

the church and the moral leaders need to be seen and heard listening to the world

one could argue that it is a hopeful sign of the church, in dialogue with others, receiving insights from other leaders and building a relationship with the world.

I think both these are sets of seeds in the ground. Either way, there is plenty of evidence that Christianity is not a spent force when it comes to current moral debates. Even when Cardinal Cormack Murphy-O'Connor let slip at a meeting with priests in Leeds that he thought Christianity in Britain was 'almost vanquished', the media reaction ironically told a different story.

If Christianity was anywhere near vanquished, his comment would not have got on to the front pages of national newspapers and into the columns of the leader-writers!

In an essay on the moral theology of Michael Banner, called 'Journey into the World Before Turning it Upside Down',[4] Richard Harries, the Bishop of Oxford, writes about the Christian natural-law tradition. He argues that, although many modern philosophers reject it as meaningless and mistaken, it merits revision and attenuation. He makes three points. First, it is self-evident that human beings exhibit the capacity to make moral judgments and the ability to distinguish right and wrong.[5] Secondly, 'despite real differences between cultures, religions and ideologies and despite all the moral fragmentation we associate with a postmodern world, it is in fact possible to achieve some degree of consensus about basic values and moral issues'.[6] Thirdly, 'our human moral awareness and capacity for some degree of moral consensus is [*sic*] God-given'.[7] Creation as well as salvation express God's grace. Richard Harries develops his argument to challenge the Barth/Banner position that there is 'an unbridgeable gap between Christian ethics and all other ethical systems'.[8] Without going into detail, I am with the Bishop, not just on the grounds of episcopal collegiality, but because I see intuitions of this position in Scripture, and because such an approach provides a way forward for Christians to offer leadership in the multilingual ethical debates that affect our multicultural globe.

Scriptural and self-evident

If we look more closely at the four principles of moral awe, we find that they are all rootable and explicit in Scripture, while at the same time being recognizable (at least the first three) by anyone today as self-evident and empirically valid.

First, 'all our actions spring from and shape our characters'. It was Jesus, admittedly in a different context, who said, 'What comes out of you is what makes you "unclean". For from within, out of your hearts, come evil thoughts ... ' (Mark 7:20–21 NIVI).

Secondly, 'all our actions have consequences, individually and socially'. Paul, following the emphasis in Jesus' own teaching about the judgment of God, wrote: 'Do not be deceived: God cannot be mocked. People reap what they sow. Those who sow to please their sinful nature, from that nature will reap destruction ... ' He uses this as an encouragement to live a morally good life: 'Let us do good to all' (Gal. 6:7–8, 10 NIVI).

Thirdly, 'all our actions will be judged by future generations'. Judgment (Greek, *krisis*) held before us in the word 'crisis', is not a fashionable or politically correct notion, but it is clearly present in Scripture in terms of God's creation of a world where actions have consequences and causes have effects. The Bible says uncomfortably but truthfully that God 'punishes the children for the sin of the fathers to the third and fourth generation' (Num. 14:18).

This sounds cruel and unfair. But the fact is that we do bear the wounds of previous generations, as surely as our succeeding generations will bear the marks of our own folly. For example, two hundred years on, in Liverpool we still bear the scars of the slave trade, with marginalized ethnic communities and endemic racism. In years to come, our children's children will, no doubt, evidence the effects of our liberal poisoning of the oceans.

Fourthly, 'all are responsible for our actions to whatever or whoever is the source of our moral intuition'. Jesus' most compelling picture was of the Day of Judgment, when we shall all stand together with the least, last and lost and will bear his scrutiny: 'I tell you the truth, whatever you did not do for one of the least of these, you did not do it for me' (Matt. 25:45).

This is the clearest expression of accountability. The Lawgiver is met in both the action and the inaction, in both the beloved and the neglected. The source of our moral intuition meets us whether our eyes are closed or open to recognize him.

The point of this briefest of expositions is that there is a biblical basis to each of the hallmarks of moral awe, yet none of them requires an acceptance of biblical authority in matters of faith and conduct to commend itself to people of other faiths or no faith.

An example: the environment

Let us, in conclusion, take a contemporary example, which has at its base an ethical foundation. How ought we to treat the planet? In particular, let us focus on the issue of climate change and the contentious point that this is related to carbon emissions into the atmosphere. How do we proceed? How do the four principles of moral awe steer us both in the debate and in the decision-making process?

> *to desecrate creation is not just a crime against humanity, but ultimately a blasphemy, for it is to undo the creative work of Christ*

First, 'all our actions spring from and shape our characters'. The release of carbon into the atmosphere is to do with consumption, and the excessive release (on average 2–4 tons per person per year in Britain) is to do with excessive consumption. (In America the average per year is 5 tons per person. Ecological balance requires an average of 0.4 tons per person annually.) We are individually responsible for our lifestyle and we are shaped by our indulgence.

Secondly, 'all our actions have consequences, individually and socially'. The degree of increase in emissions, coupled with the massive deforestation that destroys the lungs of the earth, is a matter of dispute among scientists and how it is affecting the ozone layer, climate change and sea levels. Some say that Earth, like the human body, has the capacity to heal itself and restore the balance; others believe that we may be heading for a point of no return. Either way, the fact is that the actions are not without consequences. We may not see them immediately, but even in our own lifetime we start to reap what we sow.

Thirdly, 'all our actions will be judged by future generations'. We judge our forebears with ease, and with all the gall and guile of the friend searching for the speck in his friend's eye while a plank sticks out of his own. We look back with incredulity, and wonder how on earth they could have justified their actions. For example, how could Christians have acquiesced in the slave trade and slavery? Yet it is a salutary exercise to speculate what our successors will wonder about us with greater incredulity in a hundred years' time. Perhaps they will form a view of our failure to work out a just and universal system for the use of carbon.

Fourthly, 'we are all responsible for our actions to whatever or whoever is the source of our moral intuition'. The Christian sees this explicitly as a call to be accountable to the Creator. According to the New Testament (John 1:1–3; Col. 1:16; Heb. 1:1–3), all things come into being through and for Christ. This means that to desecrate creation is not just a crime against humanity, but ultimately a blasphemy, for it is to undo the creative work of Christ.

The future of the planet is precarious. It requires courageous leadership, nationally and internationally, in both politics and commerce. It requires moral leadership, which entails listening, learning, telling and teaching people how it is, how it will be and how it *ought* to be.

Leaders need to live by the four principles of moral awe and to encourage others to see and recognize the moral imperative to act accordingly. Why? For two reasons. First, because that is the very nature of things. Secondly, because we stand on the edge, the cliff crumbling beneath our feet, the earth 'slip-sliding away' into very troubled waters.

RESPONSE
by Andrew Goddard

Since Paul Simon is high among my favourite singer-songwriters, the brilliantly evocative title of this third chapter immediately grabbed my attention, and the chapter itself raises a great number of important ideas. It has once again spurred me to go back and think through some theological and ethical issues and to reread parts of Scripture.

Three 'M's, and a fourth

The first chapter mentioned that this third chapter would suggest a proposition as to how Christianity might speak the language of moral conviction into a diverse and pluralistic culture. At the heart of this project is the concept of moral awe. Before exploring that idea further, I want to step back and try to look at the bigger picture. Although not unsympathetic to the proposal, I believe that unless such an account is set in the right context, and unless its rationale is clear, it could lead the church in the wrong direction and distort the moral leadership the church should be offering.

Early on, the chapter returned to review the troubled waters we find in contemporary culture. These can undermine attempts at moral leadership, and certainly are factors Christian leaders must recognize when putting forward their moral views or engaging in moral debate. The first of the three 'M's, the media, I discussed in some detail in my response to the first chapter. I share its concerns at the effect of much of the media on the structure and character of moral argument in our country.

The second 'M', the market, clearly correlates with the idol of consumerism in chapter 1. It is a most disturbing feature of our life at the start of the twenty-first century that the human phenomenon of the market has (like every good that becomes a god) extended its important but limited role in economic life to take over as much of life as it can. In relation to moral leadership and debate, it now functions in a number of ways. As we have already seen, there is now a supermarket of moral opinions, which threatens to reshape how we think about moral questions. There is also now an apparent unwillingness to allow morals to prohibit, or even to limit and control, the marketing of products and services. To oppose on moral grounds (and certainly to seek to legislate against) practices for which (it appears) there is both supply and demand within society increasingly feels like trying to prevent the tide from coming in, for to do so is understood to deny individual freedom and the freedom of the market.

Related to this is the third 'M', multiculturalism. This (like 'establishment') is a rather slippery term, and its ambiguity is often unhelpful, leading to confusion in moral debate and problems for moral leaders. I recently heard the contrast expressed in terms of a choice between fruit purée and fruit salad. In the 'purée' model, 'multiculturalism' easily becomes tied to a strongly pluralist and relativist ideology. This, far from being truly multicultural, seeks to establish its own cultural dominance by seeking to eliminate distinctiveness among other cultures (bananas, apples and pears are all mashed togther). This 'multiculturalism' is at least unsettled by, if not outright hostile to, any subcultures in society that seek to maintain a firm and distinctive moral identity, or, worse still, to critique and seek to transform other cultures. The paradoxical situation then arises when, in the name of multiculturalism, certain cultures are prevented from being themselves, and a (usually secular, technocratic, 'liberal') imperialistic monoculture is imposed.

In contrast, the 'fruit salad' model of multiculturalism represents something the Christian church should welcome in its recognition and respect for distinctive variety and 'flavours' (apples remain apples, alongside pears, which remain pears). The church, after all, is called to be the multicultural community,

> *the church, after all, is called to be the multicultural community*

and our vision of the end of history includes 'a great multitude ... from every nation, tribe, people and language' (Rev. 7:9). Defending this vision of the end is part of what Paul is doing in his insistence that justification is not by works of the law. The church here and now is, in other words, not simply to impose Jewish culture on to the Gentile world.

The church has, of course, sadly often failed to realize the full implications of this great vision of the redeemed community. Even Christians who place great stress on the Pauline doctrine of justification by faith are often blind to their cultural imperialism. On the mission field we have often imposed Western culture as 'Christian', and, at home, a particular culture (predominantly middle-aged, middle-class) often dominates and identifies our churches. The church should, however, welcome genuine multi-culturalism. It should do so within its own walls, as members of the varied cultures of society are drawn to Christ and as they discern, through worshipping the triune God together, what in their different cultures reflects God's good creation restored in Christ and what is a sign of the distorting power of sin.[9] It should also welcome multiculturism outside the church, in society, and should beware of any culture (even, and perhaps especially, a tolerant liberal one) that seeks hegemony and control. In particular, it must not allow those who are opposed to the church's claims or cautious about all explicitly religious cultures so to emphasize diversity that, as James puts it, it 'feels like some-one tugging and pulling the moral carpet from beneath our feet'. There are, as the chapter emphasizes, many areas in which the main religious traditions in our country share a common moral vision, and we must not be frightened of drawing atten-tion to that, and, where possible,

> *Christians who place great stress on the Pauline doctrine of justification by faith are often blind to their cultural imperialism*

of working together to persuade others of our conception of the good life. In January 2001, for example, it was important that Christian, Jewish, Muslim and Sikh leaders wrote an open letter to the House of Lords, asking that proper scrutiny be given before agreeing to extend legal boundaries on embryo research.

Examples such as that would lead nicely into the central proposal of the chapter, but first I want to suggest a fourth 'M' that is also of great importance: 'mastery'. Part of what we witness in the world today as a direct challenge to much moral thinking is humanity's use of power to take control and impose its will on the world. This is what lies behind the environmental crisis on which the chapter concentrates, and also, of course, behind so many issues in medical ethics.

As Christians we must, as so often, see a fundamental truth in this attitude within the world, because Scripture reveals to us that we humans are indeed made by God to rule over God's creation. The real problem, however, is that our contemporary (post)modern world has ripped this understanding out of its wider context in the Christian story. In particular, our quest for mastery refuses to recognize three limits that are placed on this mastery, according to Scripture. First, since the fall, we are destined for suffering and death: 'by the sweat of your brow you will eat your food until you return to the ground, since from it you were taken; for dust you are and to dust you will return' (Gen. 3:19). We cannot rescue ourselves from this curse, but we do not need to do so, for God has done so in Jesus Christ and his suffering and death. Secondly, as that verse in Genesis reminds us, we are set over creation as an integral part of it; we return to the ground, from which we were taken. We must, therefore, respect and rejoice in God's good gift and ordering of his world and not seek to impose our own wills upon it. To act in ignorance or violation of God's ordering of creation is to increase the disorder and deformity of the fallen world. Thirdly, we are called to rule the world as 'the image of God', and that means under the wise and loving rule and reign of God and his moral law, not as autonomous controllers. We are to see ourselves simply as tenants in the vineyard (cf. Luke 20:9ff.). And, of course, if we want to know what it means to be and to rule as the image of God, we look to Christ, 'the image of the invisible God' (Col. 1:15). The mastery of this true Lord is one of service (Mark 10:42–45). It stands in sharp contrast to the mastery of our world, because 'The god of this age has blinded the minds of unbelievers, so that they cannot see the light of the gospel of the glory of Christ, who is the image of God' (2 Cor. 4:4).

In the face of this fourth 'M', one of the most appealing features of this chapter's account of moral awe, to me, is that it would engender in leaders the virtue of humility, in contrast to the pride and power that are so predominant at present.

Another look at Paul in Athens

Before commenting on the 'bridge' of moral awe outlined here, I want to trace how I understand James's development of them, and raise some questions and possible modifications to what I think he is proposing. The two building-blocks of his proposal are a belief in moral objectivity (like the tree in the Oxford Quad, moral law or moral order exists whether or not we pay attention to it) and a recognition of the universality of moral awareness and moral language, which remain strong in our culture despite all the moral confusion and talk of pluralism and relativism.

Both of these are, I think, important points, which the Christian moral tradition has spoken of in such terms as 'natural law' and 'conscience', appealing to texts such as Romans 1:18ff. and 2:13ff. for an apostolic authorization for such beliefs. In relation to the first, I am fully in agreement in relation to what has been termed 'Christian moral realism'. I am, however, uncertain whether James places too much faith in the second building-block – a general moral sense – as a means of accessing moral truth, and whether this leads to giving this supposed common 'bridge' too foundational a place in Christian moral thinking and leadership.

The argument self-consciously draws an analogy with Paul's practice in Athens according to Luke in Acts 17: 'What I propose to identify is a latter-day Athenian altar. Paul identified an altar in Athens as a bridge between what the philosophers believed and what he had been destined to proclaim.' The chapter seeks to trace and follow the significance of 'Paul's method of finding common ground in their aspirations, their symbols and their literature'. The aim here, as I understand it, is to take what Paul did in relation to the Athenians' spiritual sense and quest for God, and to try to do something similar in relation to contemporary society's moral sense and quest for the Good. Although there are dangers and limits in this – what Paul did in Athens is not the only (or probably even the major) strategy in his mission – it potentially offers us great insight and reward in our increasingly pagan culture. My reading of Acts 17:16ff. would lead me to draw the following lessons, some of which I sense to be in tension with James's approach as he seeks to establish a 'moral bridge over troubled waters'.

First, Paul was distressed by what he saw in this great city of the ancient world, for it was 'full of idols' (verse 16). So today, we perhaps need to feel the same sort of distress about the idolatry of our society, which we began to analyse in chapter 1 and returned to in this chapter. And, of course, as the whole of Scripture makes clear (not least Rom. 1), idolatry leads to immorality. The injustices and social breakdown we see around about us, and the moral confusion in people's minds, should therefore cause us distress. They should lead us to think seriously about how to respond and to look for godly, moral leadership that will address these issues by discerning and challenging our idols and pointing us back to the true God.

Secondly, Paul therefore turns to reason with both the gathered people of God and the wider world (verse 17). By analogy, as Christians, our distress at the situation we find in our society should first of all lead us to share our moral vision and lines of moral reasoning. We should do this both with those who are most amenable to them (the church and perhaps, by extension, with other faith communities, especially, like Paul here, with the Jews) and with anyone else who is interested.

Thirdly, and this is most important, whoever we speak to, we seek to persuade them in terms of the gospel we have received (verse 18). Those who were not regulars at the synagogue – the Epicurean and Stoic philosophers – were drawn into dispute, and did not instantly understand, because 'Paul was preaching the good news about Jesus and the resurrection'.

In relation to moral leadership and moral debate today, we first and foremost need this same confidence in the gospel message. It is this same good news about Jesus and the resurrection (and not any subsequent bridge that we might be able to build) that has to be the rock on which we unashamedly stand, even if this leads us into dispute with those who do not share these beliefs and who might therefore accuse us of simply 'babbling' (see verse 18).

Fourthly, as a result of this gospel-based persuasion, Paul was invited on to their territory to discuss things further (verses 19–21). Again, this may strike us as strange, but it is the very fact that Paul was saying something distinctively different ('new teaching . . . strange ideas . . . ') that provided him with a platform on which to present his case. Undoubtedly, Christian moral leaders today can face a handicap in that, unlike the Athenians, many people think they already know what the church has to say on any issue, or believe they hold 'Christian values'. On many issues, however, they do not really know, or they think they know but they are wrong, or, possibly in the majority of cases, even if they do know and are right, they do not really know *why* Christians have the moral beliefs they do.

Fifthly, when invited on to their ground, Paul found a point of contact (verses 22–23). Here, for some reason, is where we often think we must begin – finding the altar to the unknown God. All the evidence suggests, however, that, although this was a crucial part of Paul's strategy, it was not what Paul had been saying until now. It is also important to see the nature of this 'point of contact'. What Paul did was to take part of the evidence that distressed him when he looked carefully at their culture. The part he takes is the point at which he found a sign that revealed their weakness and ignorance and limits. He then pointed this out to them and offered to shed light on their darkness: 'what you worship as something unknown I am going to proclaim to you' (verse 23).

If we pursue the analogy into the moral sphere, we see that it is necessary to look carefully at the moral discourse of the world to find where that moral discourse breaks down (either implicitly or explicitly) or where it cannot give a proper account of what it is doing because its true moral claims require the gospel to make sense. That could take various forms. It might mean taking cases where society struggles to explain its use of the language of 'good' or 'happiness'.[10] It may mean drawing society's attention to the incoherence of its view of life in the womb when we abort millions and yet seek to generate life in a test tube and do all we can to ensure a healthy pregnancy when there is a 'wanted child'. It may mean asking why, if everyone has the right to die, we can ever justifiably limit euthanasia only to patients in certain extreme situations. Whatever the analogies might be, they are certainly not seeking a common, agreed, universal foundation on which we can then build.

Sixthly, having drawn attention to this evidence of their failure to grasp reality properly, Paul then preaches the gospel to them. He does this in a way that, although it uses some of their own language, is fundamentally critical of their whole way of life and calls for them to turn from it (verses 24–31). He has promised to tell them what they do not know, and he does so in an unashamedly Jewish manner: there is one creator God, who has no time for their various apparently wonderful religious enterprises but whom they need to obey and with whom they need to be in relationship, and who has appointed Jesus as judge.

Again, the analogy is interesting when we shift from the religious quest for God to the moral quest for the Good. We need to make known the basic features of the Christian story that are given to us in Scripture, and to explain what these tell us about the moral order and our calling as humans to live in God's world as his image-bearers. We need to be critical of the various human attempts to define and establish the Good apart from God, for, as Dietrich Bonhoeffer famously reminds us in the opening sentences of his *Ethics*, this is actually – like the idols and altars of Athens – a sign that we have got everything wrong: 'The knowledge of good and evil seems to be the aim of all ethical reflection. The first task of Christian ethics is to invalidate this knowledge ...'[11]

Like the poets and philosophers Paul cites, we shall find that the world's moral leaders do know something of moral truth. We need not deny that, and we can and should use examples of this in addressing our modern-day Areopagus meetings, whether in the media or in the pub. But these are never sought out to provide us with a common starting place on which we hope we can then build a Christian moral message. They are signs of what some in the Reformed tradition call 'common grace', which can be used as occasional illustrations when, like Paul, we seek to proclaim what our audience does not truly know. They are not a firm foundation on which to stand and build together but rather shaky edifices which can point people to the need for deeper truths about God and ourselves that only the gospel provides.

there is a danger that we think we must win all the arguments

Seventhly, Paul received a mixed response (verses 32–34). Again, this is an important lesson for moral leaders today. There is a danger that we think we must win all the arguments, or even that we are called somehow to establish our moral views in secular law. Often it is the desire to do this that tempts us to back-pedal on being distinctively Christian in the presentation of our case. We perhaps think that if only we translated everything into other people's way of thinking, or at least carved out an agreed set of foundational beliefs and moral principles, we would be able to win them over to our position. Paul, as I have tried to show, did not do that at Athens.

I find myself much more on the side of Barth and Banner than of my own bishop, Richard Harries, with whom James's sympathies lie. I believe that this position is supported by a careful reading of both Acts 17 and other parts of Scripture. Paul's method in Athens actually proves much less conducive than is commonly thought to a strategy that seeks 'a common *modus operandi*'. It does not set out to build 'a bridge ... [that] enables the Christian to stand on common ground with the world'. It does not look for ground that is 'self-evident' but not derived from God's self-revelation in Christ. It does not seek principles which do not require an acceptance of biblical authority.

Common ground or common question?

Where does that leave me and my reaction to James's proposal of rediscovering moral awe? Near the start of the chapter he describes his quest as one for 'some common moral ground on which we might all stand – Christian, theist, those of other faiths, atheist, humanist and agnostic'. He pictures two alternatives to this proposal – retreating in despair into a holy huddle, or bunkering down in a battle with occasional rescue missions on enemy territory. I want to try, rather tentatively, to carve out something else, which is near to James's model but also significantly different.

I think there is not so much a common moral ground that we need to mark out, as a common moral question that we are all seeking to answer. This could be expressed in various ways, but one is 'How shall we therefore live?' All are struggling with this question, whatever their faith, whether they are serving the living God or some idol(s). We all approach it differently, however, because of that word 'therefore', which shows that answering how we are to live comes out of a wider perspective on life, a larger narrative that we tell. Some of our analysis in this book has been to discern what that narrative is in the modern world. One way of thinking of this bigger picture is in terms of worldviews and worldview questions. Tom Wright, in his work on the historical Jesus, has expressed these as 'Who are we? Where are we? What's wrong? What's the solution? What time is it?'[12] Whether or not we accept this particular formulation of the questions, differences at this more fundamental level often explain both why we disagree over the ethical question of how we are to live and why we disagree so passionately.

But if that is the common question, and if our approaches to it are shaped by other deeper questions, I want to maintain that Christians have to refocus that common question in the light of the response to those deeper questions. At the heart of the Christian faith is the belief that, because of our sin, we cannot answer those deeper questions by ourselves, but that God has answered them for us in the gospel of Jesus Christ. When we turn to the specifically moral question, we find the Christian calling expressed in terms such as these: 'I urge you to live a life worthy of the calling you have received' (Eph. 4:1); 'live a life worthy of the Lord' (Col. 1:10); and 'conduct yourselves in a manner worthy of the gospel of Christ' (Phil. 1:27).

The moral question for Christians is not, then, the more general 'How shall we therefore live?' but rather 'How shall we therefore live lives worthy of our calling and of the gospel of Christ?' And, for all the reasons discussed earlier, about the gospel as public truth that restores all creation, and the lordship of Christ as over all the world, the Christian cannot believe that this is just the peculiar Christian form of the more general question, which yields answers valid only for Christians. Asking this more focused question is, in fact, the only assured way of getting the answer to the broader human question of how we are to live our lives. To seek some common, agreed strategy for answering the broader question which cannot recognize that that question has been reconfigured by God through his answer in the gospel, is therefore in danger of building on sand rather than on rock.

What does all that mean in practice? It means, I think, that the first (but certainly not the only) concern of Christian moral leadership has to be to enable the church, as the community of the baptized, who worship the triune God and follow Jesus, to answer that question of how to live lives worthy of the gospel: to answer it not only with our minds but with our flesh, not only intellectually but incarnationally. And that answer is, of course, to be given in the world and for the world, not withdrawn from the world. That answer is what will make the church salt and light and a city set on a hill (Matt. 5:13ff.).

If the church and her leaders are doing that, then, as with Paul's preaching in Athens, it will produce questions and puzzlement and a desire for explanation on the part of those who are asking the universal moral question. The way we answer in relation to our money, our property, our marriages, our families, our care for the poor, our quest for justice and our response to sickness will be noticed in the wider world and will have an impact. When called on to explain it, we must not hide the fact that we live this way in response to the work of God and to his call in Jesus Christ, and that it is accomplished by the power of his Spirit.[13] But we need not deny that our lives, which seek to be worthy of the Lord, have resonances and similarities with other ways of living life. The fact that the call of God begins in creation, the witness of the wisdom literature in the Old Testament, and some of the surface parallels between Graeco-Roman moral codes and New Testament ethical teaching, should lead us to expect to be able and willing to make connections. Those outside the church have gained insights, even if their answer about how to live is not self-consciously shaped by the gospel.

we can still learn from those whose worldviews are different from our own something of what it means to live as God made us to live in his world

What is more, as this chapter reminds us on a number of occasions, the church (despite listening regularly to the word of God in the gospel) has sometimes failed to hear the voice of God, whereas some outside the church can bear witness to God's reign. The chapter's emphasis on dialogue, listening and learning is of vital importance, as we can still learn from those whose worldviews are different from our own something of what it means to live as God made us to live in his world.

It is here, and in this context, that the principles of moral awe set out in this chapter ('at least the first three', as James himself more cautiously notes at one point) are, I believe, important; not because they provide a bridge on which Christians are to stand in solidarity with others, but because they describe some crucial features of all human action. They are, therefore, essential features in formulating responses to that first, broadest, universal moral question. They are, as the chapter shows, also insights to which Scripture bears witness in a number of ways. They can and must, therefore, be brought to bear on all thinking about and discussion of how we are to live, and they must be part of the moral formation of children in our education system. Indeed, the first principle that all our actions spring from and shape our characters is prominent in one of the best sets of stories relating to moral formation and education – the Harry Potter series. At the end of the second book, Dumbledore impresses on Harry, 'It is our choices, Harry, that show what we truly are, far more than our abilities.'[14] The principles of moral awe can and must act as critical evaluative tools in examining proposals on specific moral issues, as this chapter illustrates with reference to the environment. In fact, although I have not seen them laid out in this way before, it is hard to see how any attempt at moral discourse that failed to acknowledge them could be considered morally serious.

And yet the principles of moral awe remain, to my mind, more procedural than substantive and more general than specific. They very helpfully summarize some of the inescapable moral realities that we ignore at our peril, because they are, as James says at the end, 'the very nature of things'. They are sufficiently broad that many who are not Christians will indeed be able to subscribe to them. However, as moral laws relating to human action compared to scientific laws, they work at the level of saying that if you throw something up it will come down. They remind us that what we do reveals something about us and has an effect on us (character) as well as having an impact on others (consequences), who will have an opinion on what we have done (children). All that is not insignificant in setting a framework of moral dialogue and debate in our confused context. The very fact that these things do concern us, that there is some sense of awe, is itself important and, like the altar to the unknown god, should provoke us to ask questions – why do these things matter to us and how do we make sense of this reality of our world? Nevertheless, these principles are not the equivalent of more complex scientific laws that tell us how high something will go given the force with which it is tossed into the air or how quickly it will land again. In other words, they are not precise enough to tell us exactly what the effects of any particular action will be or, more importantly, how to identify the good by which we evaluate character, consequences or the yet unknown judgment of future generations. In order to do that and so reach concrete moral judgments we need something more – a bigger story, a worldview – and that can only be the revelation of the gospel of Jesus Christ who announces, 'like a bridge over troubled water, I will lay me down'.

4

THE MORAL OF THIS STORY?
JESUS

INTRODUCTION
by Paul Boateng MP

There is a very important tradition of discussion and debate in the area around the Palace of Westminster where the lectures that form this book were delivered. That tradition is a vital part of our nation's intellectual as well as Christian life. In the seventeenth century, at the height of the Cromwellian revolution, a great preacher by the name of John Preston preached in the area at a time when the nation had what was described as a 'Parliament of the Saints'. In this day and age we certainly do not have a Parliament of the Saints, Parliamentarians who would wish to be described as such. But, like today, the seventeeth century was a time of great uncertainty and challenge; there was fearfulness abroad and at home, and a clash of ideas. Preston addressed one group of people who had gathered around Westminster, anxious to be involved in the debate and in all that was going on. He cried out to them, 'Ye must be men and women of contention!' Paul himself enjoined us to 'contend for the faith that was once for all entrusted to the saints' (Jude 3).

James Jones is a man of contention, who, throughout his ministry, has not been afraid of ideas or of the clash of ideas, and who has, through rigorous intellect and inspirational leadership, contributed not only to the growth, strength and ideas within our church and our faith, but also significantly, to practical action that makes a difference to people's lives, particularly the lives of the least advantaged, the poorest and the most oppressed. He has contributed to their lives through championing the cause of regeneration – not only spiritual regeneration, but also the regeneration of the fabric of society in every sense of that term, in housing, in jobs and real-life opportunities.

It must be our hope, as Christians at this time, that we will see a revival of thinking, discussion and debate around ideas that have at their source the love of God and the life of our Lord. So it gives me great pleasure to introduce the fourth and final chapter in this book, focusing now on Jesus as moral leader.

THE MORAL OF THIS STORY?
JESUS
by James Jones

Feet of clay

In classic English understatement, Iris Murdoch, one of the great
novelists of the human condition, wrote, 'if one appeals to the
general notion of human nature, must one not agree that we are
on the whole not framed to be particularly good?'[1] This led her to
conclude, 'Government should legislate with human frailty in
mind.'[2]

It is a Christian insight that human beings, while retaining the
capacity for virtue, are essentially flawed and fall short of the moral
standards of God. None is perfect. This immediately presents a
challenge for all who aspire to moral leadership. We all have clay
feet. We all risk being outed as hypocrites. I have heard senior

politicians say that, while they believe in the fundamental importance of marriage and in the value of the family to social cohesion, they are reluctant to go on public record and introduce these principles into public policy for fear of being set upon by the Press (and not just the tabloids) and having their relationships examined as far back as their student days. They fear not just for themselves, but for their spouses and children and for former relationships. We can all think of examples where the media have been merciless in their treatment of political and religious leaders. No doubt the first question put to the next Archbishop of Canterbury at the Press conference to announce his appointment will be 'Did you smoke pot as a student?'

private life cannot be divorced from public office

Mind you, that might be considered progress! The first question I faced when I became Bishop of Hull was 'Do you believe in God?'!

I have gone on record as saying that private life cannot be divorced from public office; that an invitation to vote for someone is an invitation to trust that person, and that the trustworthiness of a candidate is a legitimate subject of public interest. If the candidate has deceived others close to him or her in business, in the community or in his or her family, how does the electorate know that he or she will not deceive them, who are at a distance?

Although I still hold to this view, I believe it needs amplifying, and the amplification exposes something that is missing from our national life. I want to maintain the indivisibility of private life and public office, not least because to divorce the two leads people to become ever more cynical about those in public life, whom they see as just feathering their own nest. The more we divide the private from the public, the more the notion of public service evaporates.

But how do we hold together the duty to uphold certain values and virtues with the reality that we are all sinners who fall short of the glory of God and, like sheep, have turned aside and gone our own way? This is a major problem, for it is having an effect on those who are prepared to offer themselves for public service. Many shrink from the exposure and inevitable scrutiny of every part of their life. It leads some public figures to mendacity over trivial misdemeanours for fear of the media fallout, only then to find themselves later hounded out of office for the mendacity itself. The media are merciless, and the public are as unforgiving as the crowds in the Colosseum who turned their thumbs downwards on the fate of the gladiators.

Had King David lived with today's media, he would have been exposed for his adultery with Bathsheba and his collusion in the murder of her husband Uriah, and hounded from public office for ever. Like John Profumo, he would have done penance and reparation through tireless work in the East End of Jerusalem. But the rehabilitation and restoration of public figures whose fallen natures have been exposed are more problematic today, for we do not have a culture of repentance and forgiveness. It has become almost fashionable for people to issue apologies, although their lawyers ensure circumspection so as not to admit liability. And some of the apologies are illusory. 'I'm sorry you felt hurt' is a very different sentiment from 'I'm sorry that I've hurt you.' The latter is genuine remorse; the former simply adds blame to the aggrieved for being so offended.

But while there are expressions of sorrow, what our society is deprived of, through its diminished experience of Christianity, is a mechanism of public forgiveness. An individual may well find forgiveness personally both from those he has offended and from God, but restoration and rehabilitation to public life are more difficult, because there is no commonly held mechanism whereby our society can express forgiveness and absolution. Thus, a public figure can go to prison and come out with his conviction spent, and yet still find the media and the public merciless and unforgiving and determined to bar him for ever from public office.

Grace and truth

In chapter 3 I made a call for a recovery of moral awe to accompany all our decision-making; in this chapter I draw attention to the need for moral leaders to challenge the prevailing and censorious mood of the media, and to breathe into public life and public policy the twin principles of justice and mercy. In today's world there is much borrowing of religious language and imagery – mission statements, leadership with vision, evangelistic salesforces, born-again cars and the cool use of 'Bless' in the youth culture. Whereas vision in management and politics is invariably about objectives, goals and strategies, vision in the Bible is exclusively of God. The vision that moral leaders, influenced by Scripture, are to have is of God, whose love issues in justice and mercy. It is the character of God that is to be the model of the quality of our society. A world of justice alone is a very cruel place for sinners to find themselves in. We are all left gasping for the oxygen of forgiveness. Moral leadership in the New Testament has the hallmarks of justice and mercy.

William Temple, one of Anglicanism's greatest social theologians, is reported to have said of himself that he felt most at home in the Gospel of John. So do I. In the opening chapter we read, 'The law came through Moses; grace and truth through Jesus Christ' (John 1:17). As Grace and Truth incarnate, he walked the face of the earth as pastor and prophet, demonstrating in practical ways the compassion of God and urging on the world the justice of God. The loveliest (and I use the word consciously) example of this is to be found in the eighth chapter of John. The religious and moral leaders made a woman caught in adultery stand before Jesus and a crowd of people in the temple. (Where, by the way, was the man?) When Jesus challenged them about their own private lives, they began to drop the stones – or at least to walk away. Notice, John tells us that the older ones left first – the young, more idealistic, held on, more ready to condemn; the older ones, more realistic, knew that there but for the grace of God went they. When eventually it was just the two of them, the voice of the pastor spoke: 'neither do I condemn you', then the voice of the prophet: 'Leave your life of sin' (8:11).

Notice the order. The pastor precedes the prophet. Had the prophetic word pointing up the Commandments come first, she may not have been there to hear the pastor speak of God's compassion. Both grace and truth must characterize the moral leader. Justice and mercy, commandment and compassion, truth and grace. These are the virtues that flow from the love of God. It is vitally important to hold these virtues together. The truth is that I could not continue as a Christian, let alone as a leader within the church and society, if I did not embrace and was not embraced by the mercy, compassion and forgiveness of God as well as by his Commandments.

both grace and truth must characterize the moral leader

Leaders too are learners

At the same time as acknowledging the reality of human nature and the inherent weakness of all moral leaders, we need also to recognize that no leader can be omniscient, especially in such a complex world. There is a continual pressure on those in leadership to pronounce on all sorts of subjects, and there is little space for someone to say, 'I don't know,' or, worse still 'I'm afraid I got it wrong.' These are seen as body-blows to the leader's authority. But why? Perhaps we live in such a rapidly changing world, with frightening prophecies of doom, that we long to be guided by authoritative leaders into a secure future. We are glad to welcome new heroes to the stage, but quickly boo them off when they cease to lead us where we want to go or when they reveal their true and faded colours or when they cease to entertain us.

The time has come to say that leaders are also learners. One of my favourite cartoons is of a candidate kneeling before a bishop to be confirmed. On his back is pinned an L-plate. Look closely and you will see that an L is also woven into the bishop's mitre. Both are learners, both are disciples. I have been told that this cartoon was copied and used in a parish, and that the L in the bishop's mitre was air-brushed out. What view of leadership does that convey? What does it say about the relationship between leader and led, the leader and young people? A moral leader does not possess all the answers. They too are learning in this sophisticated world, seeking to apply moral principles to an evolving culture, whose specific moral dilemmas could never have been imagined by the authors of the Scriptures. The leader will be characterized by that recovery of moral awe, and will lead by example and with humility, urging upon us the four principles that (1) all our actions spring out of and shape our character; (2) all our actions have consequences, individually and socially; (3) all our actions will be judged by future generations; and (4) we are all responsible to whatever or whoever is the source of our moral intuition.

Of course, Christian moral leaders will be particularly conscious that the source of the moral intuition lies with God, who 'spoke ... through the prophets at many times and in various ways, but in these last days he has spoken to us by a Son' who is 'full of grace and truth' (Heb. 1:1–2; John 1:14). Christian moral leaders will keep Jesus ever before them, mindful that, having claimed 'all authority in heaven and on earth', he sent his followers off into the world to make others learners of Christ and to teach them 'to obey everything I have commanded you' (Matt. 28:18–20). The teachings are uniquely collected and expanded in the pages of the New Testament, the fuller meaning of which can be understood only by reference to the images and insights of the Old Testament.

These Testaments together form the Scriptures, which, from the earliest period of the Christian movement, were deemed 'inspired by God and . . . useful for teaching, for reproof, for correction, and for training in righteousness, so that everyone who belongs to God may be proficient, equipped for every good work' (2 Tim. 3:16–17, NRSV). There is no doubting here that the Bible is given for moral leadership. The way we read and interpret the Bible needs a separate book on hermeneutics! But, just as the recovery of moral awe has a humbling effect on decision-makers, so the placing of oneself beneath the authority of Jesus through engaging submissively with the Scriptures does its own unique work in our lives, as we seek to apply the law of God in a manner that is both gracious and truthful.

Wolfhart Pannenberg argues that our personal spirit, that which is truly and essentially oneself, cannot bow before anything except a moral personality. He quotes Wilhelm Hermann: 'Consequently the revelation of God to which we submit can be nothing else than the moral personality in which Jesus confronts us.'[3]

When it comes to expressing his mind fully and articulating his own moral character, God goes further than the prescriptions of the law of Moses. Ultimately, he gives us himself. When we ask to be shown the Truth, he answers by giving us not a set of abstract propositions but a true person, 'full of grace and truth'. 'For the law was given through Moses; grace and truth came through Jesus Christ' (John 1:17). One of the most poignant ironies in the Gospel of John is Pilate, the political leader, faced with the moral dilemma of what he should do with Jesus. Pilate asks him, 'What is truth?' (18:38). And the answer was staring him in the face! The question of Pilate was prompted by the assertion of Jesus that 'Everyone on the side of truth listens to me' (18:37). I believe that, standing with our society on the common ground of moral awe, we who follow Jesus must find new ways of enabling others who are open to searching for the truth to listen to the voice of Jesus. As a church in a pluralistic culture, we are more comfortable in our public discourse talking about God. Yet we must find new ways of listening to the unique and authoritative voice of Jesus without rubbishing other faith communities and pandering to the racism endemic in our society.

Although we can engage in a public discourse on moral leadership, and find common ground with people of other faiths and no faith by, for example, recovering that moral awe, the Christian takes a stand that ultimately says that we cannot separate ethics from metaphysics, or morality from spirituality, if we want to make sense of the world. Again, I am with Iris Murdoch: 'I certainly want to suggest that the spiritual pilgrimage (transformation – renewal – salvation) is the centre and essence of morality, upon whose success and well-being the health of other kinds of moral reaction and thinking is likely to depend.'[4]

But how do we exercise that moral leadership in a fragmentary yet globalized world? Following the lead of Alasdair MacIntyre, the Chief Rabbi Jonathan Sacks, Professor Robin Gill and Paul Vallely, and with a nod even in the direction of Bishops Richard Holloway and Jack Spong, but without losing my evangelical credentials (!), I want to argue, in conclusion, for a rediscovery of a biblical model of community.

Leadership and followership in community

The term 'moral leader' begs several questions. One of them may prompt the reader to ask why I have taken over three chapters to get to the point of addressing it!

'What do you mean by "leader"?' I once asked a leading management consultant for her definition of leadership. Her immediate reaction was 'Followership.' However much someone may be designated a leader, if that person does not have a following, he or she 'ain't no leader'! The very notion of leadership presupposes a group of followers. The idea of moral leadership presupposes a community that is bound together by certain values. Therefore, there can be no serious study of moral leadership without addressing the issue of community. Leadership and community are two sides of the one coin.

For the Christian, the model of community is primarily located in God's three persons in one community. The Gospel of John pulls back the curtain on this picture with a description of the three persons of the Trinity giving glory to one another. The Father gives glory to the Son, the Son to the Father, and the Spirit to the Son. By the same token, the Son receives glory from the Father, the Father from the Son, and the Son from the Spirit. Here is a community of mutuality caught up in a reciprocity of giving and receiving. Significantly, no-one gives glory to the Spirit. The door of the community is left ajar to welcome in new people. It is open for the church to join as she comes into the circle, bringing glory to the Spirit and to the Son and to the Father. Thus the community of God is not an exclusively mutual and excluding company, but including and inclusive, for ever widening the circle to embrace the church and the world.

> *leadership and community are two sides of the one coin*

Jesus the servant leader

This is the community that Jesus inaugurated with his first followers and that he both presided over and served as leader. The *locus classicus* is the episode of foot-washing in John 13, where Jesus reveals the nature of his own leadership. This is the only time he ever calls himself 'Lord'. 'You call me teacher and Lord, and you are right, for that is what I am' (13:13). He reveals his lordship verbally while, by his actions and on his hands and knees, he shows himself as a servant, doing the job that no self-respecting man would do, washing the dirt from the feet of his followers. Here is the deacon God, the servant Lord, Jesus, the same, yesterday, today and for ever in the role of a servant. This is his character, the character of the Moral Leader. It is not a phase that he goes through, but it belongs to his nature. This servant Lord will carry on serving his people when he returns (Luke 12:37). He will be a servant at the second coming as well as at the first.

The Servant Lord at the centre of heaven is seen in the book of Revelation as the Lamb upon the throne – the Lamb, the symbol of servanthood, innocent, having endured suffering; the throne, the symbol of lordship, his presiding over the community of the redeemed. And who is it that takes to himself the ministry of wiping away the tears from our eyes? The Servant Lord: God himself.

This is the character of God revealed in Jesus kneeling before his followers, picturing a radically different model of leadership. Cool and calculating, he poses the question 'Do you understand what I have done for you?' (John 13:12). He then gives them the example that they should wash one another's feet (verses 14–15). Note that he does not command them to wash the feet of others. He calls them to mutual service, to mutual ministry, to ministering to one another. That is very different. And the example he gives includes not only the episode of his washing their feet in John 13, but also the episode of his having his own feet washed by the woman in John 12:1–3. When they try to dismiss her, he is firm and stern with them. 'Leave her alone!' (verse 7).

The washer and the washed; the Servant Lord; mutual ministry; giving and receiving: this is how true community is born. The mutuality expressed between the persons of the Trinity is now mirrored in the community to which Jesus gives birth on earth. One of the last great questions of John's Gospel is set to connect Peter, the founder of the church, with the eternal *Logos*. Emphatically he is asked, 'Do you truly love me?', and emphatically he protests, 'You know that I love you' (21:15–17). The lover is loved. There is mutuality between heaven and earth, each loving and loved. Then, assured of his love, and connected to the world through Peter's love, Jesus reaches out to the church and to the world beyond: 'Feed my sheep' (verse 17). What with? With the sacrament of love, food of bread and wine. 'Feed on him in your heart by faith with thanksgiving.'

So the world is brought into communion with God, who so loved the world that he gave his only Son. This giving inspires giving, grace upon grace: mutual giving; mutual receiving; heaven and earth in one community, who is God, in whom 'we live and move and have our being' (Acts 17:28). The will of God is ever widening, embracing and including, fulfilling the plan for the fullness of time, 'to bring all things in heaven and things on earth together under one head' (Eph. 1:10).

This is the inclusive community, the kingdom of God. All community is to be measured by this community. It is within this community that Jesus serves as leader, the Servant Lord.

Jesus the authoritative leader

Community is therefore the only context for the moral leader. As John Howard Yoder and Stanley Hauerwas remind us,[5] the moral issue is not what we are to do but rather who we are to be. Clearly, one cannot rigidly divide action from being, or being from action. Nevertheless it is the moral quality of the community in which the leaders serve that authenticates their leadership. The Scriptures establish an inextricable link between being, doing and speaking. And yet the leaders, spiritual and moral, may by virtue of their calling, need to speak uncomfortably, even prophetically, to their own community, and risk ostracism, exclusion and even death. The moral authority of the leader depends on the moral quality of the community he or she serves.

In Luke 4, when Jesus expounds the Nazareth Manifesto of

Isaiah 61, and declares that God delights in those beyond the boundaries of their own community, synagogue praise turns to synagogue rage and they try to throw him off the cliff. The conflict was between exclusion and inclusion. Time and again, Jesus stands over and against his own community for being exclusive.

This is an example of Jesus both under authority and exercising authority, commissioned and commissioning, commanded and commanding. In the Gospels, nine authorities are explicitly ascribed to him: to judge, to forgive, to heal, to give life, to cast out demons, to lay down his life, to take up his life, to teach and to make disciples. 'All authority in heaven and on earth has been given to me' (Matt. 28:18). He is both under an authority that has been given to him and exercising that authority over others.

This language of authority and command, in which Barth (and Banner) trade enthusiastically, causes problems to others, such as Richard Harries, Bishop of Oxford, and especially to Bishops Richard Holloway and Jack Spong. 'The model of commander-commanded can encourage immaturity, even infantilism.'[6] Although he recognizes the place of this metaphor in Christian theology and ethics, he believes 'it cannot be used today in such a stark, unqualified manner as do Barth and Banner without at the least arousing moral questioning and more probably, moral protest'.[7]

Surely the qualification is the cross. Here the commanded-commander is culled. This is the destiny of the moral leader. A disturbing thought for all those who aspire to such leadership.

The values of the community of the kingdom of God are the two immediate commands to love God and love your neighbour as yourself. But, as Jesus found in Nazareth and on Calvary, these commands are not as universally popular as one might imagine, especially when love of neighbour embraces that beyond the perceived boundaries of the group and includes loving your enemy! Everybody loves Jesus until he shows us he loves that which we hate. Moral leadership involves courageously challenging such prejudice.

The questions will be asked, 'Are there any limits to this inclusiveness? Is there no-one in front of where we draw the line?' The example of Jesus in the Gospels is that he did draw the line, but, uncomfortably for those of us who are professionally religious, it was in front of the toes of the spiritual and moral leaders! 'Woe to you, teachers of the law and Pharisees!' (Matt. 23:13, 15, 23, 25, 27, 29). He drew the line to embrace the prostitutes, the treacherous tax collectors, the thieving shepherds, the lousy lepers, the poor, the blind, the lame, the least, the last and the lost.

Here was a new ethic to disturb the *status quo*. He was uncompromising about money, status, sex, love, forgiveness and judgment, and extravagantly generous in his compassion to those who knew they had messed up their lives. To those who dissembled in hypocrisy he issued nothing but dire warnings. But for them and all the world he died, pleading forgiveness of the good Father, which he continues to plead as our advocate in heaven.

everybody loves Jesus until he shows us he loves that which we hate

I am very conscious that in the course of these four chapters I have not touched on the range of contemporary issues. This has been deliberate. First, I was conscious that the media might easily pounce on these and distort the book. Secondly, I – for my own sake as well as for that of my readers – wanted to set out again the principles of engagement between the Christian faith and the world. I am an evangelical Anglican, which means that I am self-consciously a member of a national church and take as authorative in matters of faith and conduct the Scriptures of the Old and the New Testaments. I read these daily, and especially the Gospels, so as to hold before me, as both inspiration and example, the One from Nazareth, 'full of grace and truth'. In his image I hope to be restored day by day so that I may be neither truthless in grace nor graceless in truth. The aim of immersion in Scripture is not simply to read off verses as proof-texts but to be saturated by the Word of God, so that we have a new mind and a different attitude: 'Your attitude should be the same as that of Christ Jesus' (Phil. 2:5). Moral leadership, modelled on Jesus, should exhibit the twin virtues of grace and truth.

Justice and mission

I was very struck recently by an interview with Will Self in the journal *Third Way*. On the strength of it I bought several of Will Self's books. When I read several of his short stories in *Tough, Tough Toys for Tough, Tough Boys*, I was disturbed by the darkness of the tales. However, in conversation with Steve Turner, he rejects moral relativism in characteristically colourful language. 'It's a lot of balls to be taken in by this short-term moral-relativist perspective and to think that it solves anything. It does not solve ultimate questions of right and wrong. It evades the question of how to live the good life.' Although Self finds the idea of 'an incarnate God very difficult', he confesses to being very open to 'the idea that there is some form of power external to the phenemological world'.[8] I am tempted to plagiarize Paul at the Areopagus: 'What you identify as "power eternal" I am going to proclaim to you. The God who made the world and everything in it is the Lord of heaven and earth ... has made all nations to inhabit the whole earth ... so that men would seek him and perhaps reach out for him and find him, though he is not far from each one of us – He has set a day when he will judge the world with justice by the man he has appointed. He has given proof of this to all men by raising him from the dead' (cf. Acts 17:23–24, 27, 31).

Although many baulk at the idea of a God of judgment, it lies at the base of the question that is frequently put to Christians as they seek to engage the world with their faith: 'If there is a God, why doesn't he do something about the state of the world?' What is being invoked is a discerning God who will draw a line between the good and the bad, preserve the good and ditch all those who have added to the sum of human misery. Laying aside the important corollary 'who do you think would be left?' (which of itself points up our universal need of a just and merciful Saviour), the question is a profoundly moral one. It assumes some sort of absolute ethic by which we are justly judged. This is exactly where Paul takes the Athenians in his dialogue at the Areopagus: 'God has fixed a day on which all will be judged with justice by a man who he has appointed.' This man is Jesus. He is the moral of the story – full of grace and truth and the model of all moral leadership.

What is inescapable is that the Scriptures were, to him, formative both in his self-understanding and in his moral attitudes. 'Do not think that I have come to abolish the law or the prophets. I have come not to abolish but to fulfil' (Matt. 5:17). Anyone married to the servant leadership of Jesus has to embrace the Scriptures, for without them Jesus Christ lacks both definition and moral meaning.

These Scriptures were written in a time that could not conceive of the possibilities of the contemporary world. Yet they have baked into them moral principles that feed all generations.

Here are three biblical texts with moral tones.

Psalm 139:13–16 declares:

> For you created my inmost being;
>> you knit me together in my mother's womb.
> I praise you because I am fearfully and wonderfully made;
>> your works are wonderful,
>> I know that full well.
> My frame was not hidden from you
>> when I was made in the secret place.
> When I was woven together in the depths of the earth,
>> your eyes saw my unformed body . . .

This passage speaks not just of the sanctity of life but of the fearful and wonderful process of divine making. In the face of this when faced with such moral choices as abortion or cloning, we must be both humble and exceedingly cautious.

Colossians 1:16 tells us of Christ that 'by him all things were created; things in heaven and on earth, visible and invisible', thus emphasizing John's testimony, 'without him nothing was made that has been made' (John 1:3). Thus, as we face fundamental questions about the future of the planet in personal choices and future policy, we must be both humble and exceedingly cautious, for to exploit the planet recklessly and to plunder the Earth with greedy self-indulgence, grabbing as much as we can get, is not just a crime against humanity but a blasphemy, for it is to undo the gracious acts of God in creation.

In his first letter to Christians at Corinth (6:19–20), Paul expounds the beauty of the human body as 'a temple of the Holy Spirit, who is in you, whom you have received from God ... You are not your own; you were bought at a price. Therefore honour God with your body.' This is the foundation of sexual ethics. I have no space here to develop the link between the resurrection of the body and sexual ethics, but suffice it to say that the bodily resurrection is an affirmation of the body. It says that matter matters to God and that the sensual and sexual expression of the body is a means of glorifying God, as this text makes clear. It does not mean that anything goes. Rather, it supports the view that an awareness of one's body as the temple of God's Spirit is to be the principle that guides all sexual behaviour. It renders us humble, cautious and joyful.

Although I have taken these three scriptural texts in isolation, they are consonant with other biblical passages. Together they orchestrate a symphony, as do the prophetic demands for justice. From the prophecies of Amos to the Nazareth manifesto, God demands (that is not too strong a word) justice for the poor, asylum for the stranger and freedom for the oppressed. It will take courage to say 'no' to those in power who might want to back-pedal on our duty to love our neighbour as ourselves.

Before these divine principles, we are to order our lives with humility and caution. It will not always be easy to discern the right moral path. We live in a complex world, so much so that the notion of simplicity, I fear, verges on the heretical. In the incarnation, God was immersing himself into the complexity of the world.

In conclusion, it is salutary to observe that today's moral leaders are found in difficult places. The moral philosophers of the twenty-first century are the scriptwriters of soap operas, where today's moral dilemmas are acted out and then discussed throughout the land. The moral prophets are songwriters and singers, such as Sting, campaigning against the deforestation of the planet, and Bono, elevating Jubilee from a church-based organization into a popular mass movement. If leadership is defined by followership, then they are the leaders!

it will take courage to say 'no' to those in power who might want to back-pedal on our duty to love our neighbour as ourselves

If we bishops (and politicians) thought that we were the moral leaders of today, we often lack the following that is the very definition of leadership. The recovery of followership is the moral leader's most urgent task. Mission is therefore the concern of the moral leader. 'Go', says Jesus. 'Make others learners of Christ ... Teach all that I have commanded' (cf. Matt. 28:19–20). Mission and ethics belong together. The extent to which that light continues to shine in the darkness will depend on the moral quality of the Christian community and its fertility to give birth to a new generation of moral leaders.

Response
by Andrew Goddard

Following Christ as moral leader

This final chapter powerfully and passionately focuses our attention on what must be the heart of any Christian attempt to speak of the moral leader – a biblically based, trinitarian, theological account of leadership which, by speaking about God in Jesus Christ, shapes our vision of what it means to be a moral leader. Jesus is, to pick up the language of chapter 3, the real bridge over trouble water.

The chapter draws 'from Jesus those qualities that might characterize those who either aspire to or have projected on to them the responsibilities of moral leadership' (chapter 1) in the belief that Jesus 'is the moral of the story ... and the model of all moral leadership'. In response, I want to take this as the basic agenda and explore further some of the many themes and images in the chapter, but in a slightly different manner than before. James emphasizes that 'Christian moral leaders will keep Jesus ever before them' and that 'the Bible is given for moral leadership', and so I want to take two Gospel passages and think through how these shed light on the calling and task of any moral leader. Of course, none of us is Christ or called to be Christ. We are called to *follow* Christ and to be *like* him. We must confess that we constantly fail to follow this calling faithfully, and all of us – including leaders – must therefore always be humble learners who look to Christ and find in him, not primarily a pattern of moral leadership to imitate, but rather assurance that we are 'embraced by the mercy, compassion and forgiveness of God'.

> *none of us is Christ or called to be Christ. We are called to follow Christ and to be like him*

The two parts of the Gospel witness to Jesus as a moral leader that I want to examine in more detail provide two perspectives on different aspects of moral leadership. The first is the powerful story referred to in this chapter as illustrating the combination of grace and truth in Christ's prophetic and pastoral leadership – that of the woman caught in adultery (John 8:1–11). It particularly emphasizes the form of moral leadership I described in my first response as leadership on moral questions. It provides us with two contrasting patterns of such moral leadership, and illustrates how Jesus responded when he was put on the spot publicly with regard to a moral issue – an uncomfortable but not uncommon situation for moral leaders – and also how he guided someone with her moral struggles.

The second passage is, in contrast, one where Jesus takes the initiative as he enters Jerusalem for what will be the last week of his life before his crucifixion (Luke 19 – 21). Here we see how he seeks to lead God's people in the light of the arrival of God's kingdom in God's world. If the John 8 story powerfully illustrates James's point about the inclusive community, these chapters vividly demonstrate his warning that the limits to this inclusiveness are most clearly drawn 'in front of the toes of the spiritual and moral leaders'. In order to help us avoid being such leaders, Luke's account portrays a number of central characteristics to shape the vision and commitment of any whose moral leadership seeks to be Christlike.

Moral leadership in action

John tells the story of the woman caught in adultery as a sort of trial in which Jesus is the judge. John's trial narrative falls into five scenes. In the opening scene, Jesus is already on the public stage as a leader. He has been in the temple courts since dawn, teaching large crowds. Then, suddenly, there is a commotion, and some of the more established, officially recognized alternative moral leaders of God's people – the teachers of the law and the Pharisees – appear. They are not alone. These powerful, male religious leaders are dragging along a woman as they push through the crowds gathered around Jesus. They put her on display before everyone. She is their moral case study, and Jesus' moral leadership is to be put to the test in relation to her and the moral question about her that they want him to answer.

But first, he must be told her story. The leaders begin (for the woman, of course, cannot be permitted to tell her own story) with the simple facts of the matter: 'Teacher, this woman was caught in the act of adultery.' Then they remind him of the legal position, the Bible's teaching: 'In the Law Moses commanded us to stone such women' (verses 4–5).

These moral leaders view her not as a fellow human being, a person to be respected and cared for, but simply as one of 'such women'.

And so they get to the question Jesus is expected to answer. In the light of these facts and established moral teaching, 'Now what do you say?'

It would be fascinating to know what the crowd made of all this. Today's media would certainly have loved it, with its mix of sex and religious leaders in moral disagreement! In fact, the case seems pretty clear-cut. The woman has done something wrong, and the religious leaders understand that they are called to act as moral policemen, especially when the letter of God's Word is so clearly on their side. The more discerning observers, however, would already begin to realize that this is not all that is going on in this test of moral leadership.

Those who have raised this question 'Now what do you say?' probably think they are defending orthodoxy against a dangerous, new, liberal teacher, and giving the sort of moral leadership that God expects. But the situation is not that simple – moral leadership rarely is. She has, they say, been caught in the act of adultery. But the law they cite is clear: 'If a man commits adultery with another man's wife – with the wife of his neighbour – both the adulterer and the adulteress must be put to death' (Lev. 20:10). So, as James asked, where was the man? Why are these moral leaders so selective in their use of Scripture and their focus on 'such women'? Their clear and firm moral leadership is, perhaps, not quite as pure and holy as it would, on the surface, appear.

The prosecution having put their case and presented the evidence, we now move to scene two, where Jesus' judgment is awaited. What sort of leadership is he going to provide to the crowds in the face of such flagrant immorality? None, it would appear! 'Jesus bent down and started to write on the ground with his finger' (John 8:6b). He has been asked a clear and simple question on an important moral issue, and he ignores both it and those leaders who asked it. They keep on questioning him, but Jesus does not speak – not to them, not to the woman, not to the crowds. They must have felt even more frustrated than Jeremy Paxman in his famous *Newsnight* interview with Michael Howard, to whom, in the absence of a clear answer, he put the identical question fourteen times!

Then – scene three – Jesus does respond. What will he say? It would appear that a true moral leader of God's people has little choice, faced with a question in the form 'Moses commanded this ... what do you say?' He is, in effect, being asked whether or not he agrees with God's law! But, as so often (it is a theme that appears later, in our look at Luke's Gospel), the leadership Jesus offers is not in the form of a direct answer to the question he has been asked. Instead, he turns the tables totally: 'If any one of you is without sin, let him be the first to throw a stone at her' (verse 7).

His moral lead consists in shifting the moral focus that has been decided by others who claim moral leadership. The accusers are now in the dock: are *they* without sin? But Jesus is not going to judge them either; they are asked to judge themselves. An amazing piece of leadership! He has not dismissed Moses, for he has invited them to throw stones as Moses commanded. Instead, he has placed them and their actions and their reading of Scripture in a new context. He has called on those who understood their moral leadership in terms of condemning others to look not at 'this woman', but at themselves – to think about what sins *they* might get caught in. He does not press his point. He does not ask them any more questions. He does not pressure them to respond. He does not even seem interested to see who will act first and what they will do. Instead, he stoops down and returns to writing on the ground. A most intriguing pattern of moral leadership!

And so the scene changes again. In scene four, those who viewed themselves as moral leaders, the woman's accusers, have heard the judgment of this teacher, and they need to act on it. Slowly, all present begin to disperse. The older and wiser ones, as James noted, go first, while the younger, more hot-headed ones are slower. It is, however, not just the leaders who disappear. The whole crowd, through whom the woman had been dragged, now follow the leaders in response to the words of wisdom and moral leadership given by Christ. The prosecution appears to have been dropped, as the accusers have withdrawn. It has been dropped because the true moral leader has made demands on all of them, which they know they cannot meet.

The story could end there, but it does not. In the fifth, final and climactic scene, the crowd has gone, the leaders have gone, and only Jesus is left – Jesus and the woman, who alone stayed with him while he kept his head down and let events take their course following his pronouncement. Jesus' form of moral leadership on the public stage, when placed on the spot, has led to a new situation. No longer is the moral issue to be a matter of public debate about a particular person. So what form does true moral leadership now take in this private, personal situation?

Jesus straightens up and looks at her. She surely knows that she is guilty, and the people's moral leaders have made quite plain what God's law demands. She is now alone before the judge, whose initial judgment she has already heard. And what does Jesus do? He builds a relationship by getting her to speak, and he does this by another favourite tactic of his – asking her a question. But, unlike the questions he sometimes asks (especially of those who claim to lead!), this is not a difficult or a trick question. It is a simple, almost comic, one: 'Woman, where are they?' The leaders who dragged you here in moral outrage; those people whose leadership consisted in humiliating you and making a spectacle of you; those people so zealous to enforce God's law; and all those they claim to lead, who have been listening to my teaching: 'Has no-one condemned you?' (verse 10).

And so, at last, the woman can be heard in this drama: 'No-one, sir' (verse 11). None of them has condemned her. None of them has done what the leaders said Moses commanded them to do. In the light of Jesus' judgment, they have all left the place of judgment. But now comes the crucial question: what will Jesus do?

At last he speaks to her about her situation: 'Then neither do I condemn you.' This is not a declaration of innocence. It is a pardon and an assurance of forgiveness. This is the sort of moral leader Jesus is for this woman who knows her sin, who has been humiliated and abused by others, and whom the law sentenced to death. The case against her has been dismissed, and she is now told to leave the place to which she has been dragged: 'Go now', like your accusers, aware of your sin, but, having heard (unlike them) the personal word of absolution, forgiven and not condemned (verse 11). She is sent back to her community by this leader – to the community that knows she is a sinner but now also knows, because of his leadership, that fundamentally she is no different from everyone else.

But that is not all he has to say. Just as his pattern of moral leadership is not prosecution but pardon, so it is not condemnation but command. Jesus' final words to her set her on a new and difficult pathway. He does not mention her specific sin. He does not suggest an alternative lifestyle. He certainly does not just tell her to avoid repeating her crime. His words have high standards that would be soul-destroying were they not prefaced by the words of pardon and declaration that there is no condemnation. 'Go now and leave your life of sin.'

Jesus shows us here what gospel-shaped moral leadership looks like. It stands in contrast to a form of moral leadership that, sadly, many expect or have experienced from the church. Some even seem to *want* the alternative model, and one can see why by imagining the headlines this public confrontation might have got when a spin was put on it by the teachers of the law: 'Adultery not condemned'; 'Prophet rejects the law'. Something like that first-century drama in the temple courts replays itself in various forms today in the television and radio studios, the Press rooms, and the office and pub discussions. It can relate to all sorts of areas, although still the issues of sexual morality – cohabitation, homosexuality, divorce – are often the focus of moral concern, on which Christians are looked to for moral leadership. The challenging and unsettling question that arises when we place ourselves in this famous story is 'Which type of moral leader are we really following when we speak out on moral issues?'

Leading through conflict to the cross

The last week of Jesus' life is the climax of a ministry of controversial moral leadership, and can be properly understood only in that light. One hallmark of that leadership has been the shocking behaviour recounted at the start of Luke 19, when Jesus enters the house of Zacchaeus, the wealthy, despised, unscrupulous and collaborating tax collector, and shares a meal with him. Many lessons for moral leaders could be drawn from the account that follows (see, e.g., 19:37–40, 48; 20:19, on the importance of followership, which James highlights), but I want to draw attention to seven lessons of particular significance for the church and for individual Christian leaders today as they seek to nurture and recognize Christlike moral leadership for the church and the world.

1. *Painful identification with people.* All that Jesus says and does in Jerusalem is prefaced by the words 'As he approached Jerusalem and saw the city, he wept over it' (19:41). This fourth chapter places great emphasis on community and on a pattern of leadership based on service and inclusion, and we see here that this is what drives Jesus as he laments over the consequences of Jerusalem's refusal of the kingdom and feels again the pain described earlier by Luke: 'how often I have longed to gather your children together, as a hen gathers her chicks under her wings, but you were not willing!' (Luke 13:34). What ensues in Jerusalem is marked by apparently constant conflict and controversy, and true moral leadership will often have to bear those same characteristics. Unless a leader's moral confrontation and disputation are rooted in painful identification, however, he or she is divorced from the call of the God whose path took the form of incarnation.

2. *The power and significance of symbolic actions.* In both Jesus' arrival in Jerusalem on a colt (19:28–40) and his entering the temple and driving out those who were selling (19:45–46), actions speak louder than words. Here, with no need for great explanations, Jesus offers a powerful moral lead and begins to mount a moral challenge to the powers that be. In and of themselves, these actions achieved very little, and yet in a deeper sense they changed everything.

That is often the case when it comes to moral leadership: small, symbolic actions can powerfully reveal injustice and inspire others to follow those who give such a lead. The memory of that lone Chinese student standing in front of the tanks as they rolled into Tiananmen Square in 1989 is still vivid. The civil rights movement in the Southern United States was born in December 1955 when Mrs Rosa Parks refused to give up her seat to a white passenger near the front of a bus in Montgomery, Alabama, and was arrested for violating the law. In 1968, in opposition to the Vietnam War, the Berrigan

it is often stories that open up moral issues for people

brothers and seven other Christians used home-made napalm to destroy service files in the car park of Cantonsville's Selective Service Board. Actions such as these, which (as these examples show) are often taken by people who are not marked out already as leaders, are powerful, prophetic revelatory forms of moral leadership.

3. *The role of storytelling.* Jesus, after his initial head-to-head with the established moral leaders (the chief priests and teachers of the law) on the question of his authority, tells the parable of the vineyard tenants (20:9–16). This is a story that, like Nathan's tale about the rich man who takes the poor man's lamb (2 Sam. 12:1–7), addresses those in power about their abuse of that power

and calls them to account. Too often we think of moral leadership in terms of telling people what they should or, perhaps more often, should not be doing – the model we saw offered in the case of the woman caught in adultery. The reality is that it is often stories that open up moral issues for people. That is partly why – at least since *Cathy Come Home* in 1966 placed the issue of homelessness on the political map – television drama and soap operas provide such a powerful moral lead in our society. It is also why so much of Scripture is narrative in form, and why preaching that tells those biblical stories and lets people place themselves within them is so often a means of moral illumination and transformation.

4. *The centrality of Scripture.* This is one of the themes to which much attention is devoted in this chapter and it is crucial in Luke 19 – 21, where we see that Jesus is, in James's words, 'saturated by the Word of God'. He understands and interprets the world through the revelation given by God in Scripture, and then lets that understanding determine his own way of life. So the symbolic actions he performs are inspired and shaped by his reading of Scripture. The triumphal entry most clearly echoes Zechariah 9:9– 10, which itself reminds people of Psalm 72. The way Luke recounts the events, however, echoes 1 Kings 1:38–48 (verse 35); 2 Kings 9:13 (verse 36); and Psalm 118:26 (verse 38), all of which point to Jesus as the king. The cleansing of the temple, similarly, is inspired by the vision of Isaiah 56:7 and the condemnation of Jeremiah 7:11, while the message of the story that follows is shaped by Psalm 118:22 (quoted in Luke 20:17), and draws its power from the imagery of scriptural texts such as Isaiah 5.

So, today, Christian moral leadership in the form of symbolic action and storytelling should not let its agenda be set simply by what is most effective or by the way those outside the church view the world. Instead, our actions and our words should arise from letting the Scriptures teach us how to view our world and how to act in it. They should, in turn, lead people back to God's Word in order that they may make sense of what we have said and done.

Scripture becomes even more prominent as the days go by in Luke's account. We can be fairly sure that the teaching Jesus gave to the crowds (19:47; 20:1) was rooted in Scripture, but later the Scriptures themselves take centre stage and become a focus of debate and conflict. At first this is on the initiative of those out to attack Jesus (20:27–38), but then, in relation to the Son of David (20:41–44), he goes on the offensive and challenges their understanding.

Whether engaging with the world or debating with fellow Christians about how we are to live our lives (and we must not forget that these arguments in Jerusalem take place within the people of God), we also need to keep the words of Scripture central in our moral thinking. Sometimes, as here, that will lead to disagreement and even dispute about what those words mean for us today, for, as James says, 'it will not always be easy to discern the right moral path'. The very structure of this book and some of its content show the importance of dialogue and differences in developing Christian responses to issues. What must remain central, however, is the conviction that Scripture should guide us, for it is given as a lamp to our feet and a light to our path (Ps. 119:105).

5. *The subversive challenge to power.* This is a central feature of the actions and words we have already mentioned. We have witnessed the arrival in Israel's capital city of the one who is heralded as king and who then disrupts the power centre of the temple and accuses its leaders of effectively being terrorists (19:46) and murderers (20:14)!

One of the patterns in Jesus' subversive challenge is the way he turns questions back upon his interrogators. Quizzed about the source of his authority, he says, 'I will also ask you a question ...' (20:3), and, when they seek to trick him by asking whether it is right to pay taxes to Caesar, he forces them to produce the idolatrous coin only to ask them whose image it bears (20:24; cf. Deut. 4:16). In the face of powerful opposition, this ability to put his challengers on the defensive and to ask awkward questions of them is a mark of Jesus' moral leadership. It is a gift the church needs to rediscover and nurture as it increasingly finds itself on the margins and in a minority, facing powerful opposition to its message in society and politics today. It is not easy to do, but it is not impossible. Stanley Hauerwas's shocking question in an argument with a medical researcher who was defending embryo experimentation – 'What if it were discovered that fetal tissue were a delicacy; could you eat it?'[9] – is a powerful example of the sort of form it could take.

pomp and ceremony, the social status and honour that surround the teachers of the law, gain them moral standing and acclaim (20:46) and easily blind people to reality

6. *The unveiling of injustice.* The symbolic exorcism of the temple, in which the money-changers are cast out (19:45), is obviously part of this revelation and challenge, and it is further explained by Jesus' words in 21:3–4, concerning the widow's gift, where he is again concerned with the temple and money. Sadly, this latter passage is often read simply as providing us with a wonderful example of sacrificial giving, whereas in fact it also represents another vital feature of true moral leadership – seeing the moral significance in small events that others easily miss, and discerning the wrong that other people do not see because they are not looking at the world in the way God does.

Just before this incident, Jesus condemned all the pomp and ceremony, the social status and honour that surround the teachers of the law, gain them moral standing and acclaim (20:46) and easily blind people to reality. He condemned these things and warned against them because he had seen the economic injustice on which they depend: 'They devour widows' houses' (20:47; cf. Jer. 7:6, a passage that also shaped his earlier disruption in the temple). Then, to prove his point, he spots one such widow, who, apparently unnoticed among all the rich people, has come to the temple treasury and 'out of her poverty put in all she had to live on' (21:4). Her giving everything to God is not Jesus' point here. Rather, he is drawing attention to the fact that the little money she has, instead of enabling her to survive, is being taken by those who claim to be leaders – partly so as to adorn this building 'with beautiful stones and with gifts dedicated to God' (21:5), and yet 'the time will come when not one stone will be left on another; every one of them will be thrown down' (21:6).

James's chapter emphasizes the importance of justice, but tends to view this in terms of judgment leading to condemnation and so in tension with mercy. This small incident at the temple treasury reminds us that, like the Hebrew prophets before him, Jesus' moral language and his vision of justice related to the harsh realities of our social, economic and political relationships and institutions, and that his moral leadership sought to uncover and confront injustice and to bring those involved in it, like Zacchaeus, to repentance.

7. *A vision of the age to come and a trust in the God who raises the dead.* Throughout these chapters we see the danger in which Jesus places himself by being this sort of moral leader. Straight after the temple incident, we find that 'the leaders ... were trying to kill him' (19:47), and throughout there are plots to arrest him and hand him over to the political power. By the end of the week, we see the truth of James's disturbing words, 'leaders, spiritual and moral, may, by virtue of their calling need to speak uncomfortably, even prophetically, to their own community and risk ostracism, exclusion and even death ... The commanded-commander is culled. This is the destiny of the moral leader.'

If that is the case, how can anyone face being a moral leader? Here, perhaps surprisingly, the (to our ears) rather strange debate about marriage and the resurrection (20:27–39) is of great importance.

In these verses, the Sadducees offer a surreal and sarcastic critique of resurrection belief rooted in an appeal to Scripture. This revolves around the practice of levirate marriage as laid down in Deuteronomy 25:5–10 and referred to in Genesis 38:8 and the story of Ruth. It is so alien to us that we easily fail to see the moral significance of all this, and to understand how Jesus' response is so fundamental to his pattern of moral leadership.

We easily miss the social implications of the Sadducees' views. They clearly believe that God intends to overcome the problems death causes in society, such as difficult and important economic and social questions to do with inheritance and family lines, through levirate marriage. A man's name will continue in this world even if he is childless, because, on his death, his 'brother shall take her and marry her and fulfil the duty of a brother-in-law to her. The first son she bears shall carry on the name of the dead brother so that his name will not be blotted out from Israel' (Deut. 25:5–6). We also miss the very personal barb that this must have been. Here are these Sadducees, quizzing this single, celibate man, on the verge of his death, about how important it is that a man's name should not be blotted out from Israel! From their perspective, he has clearly missed out on God's way of avoiding the shame and tragedy of being blotted out from Israel, which is not that of resurrection.

These leaders' reading of Scripture says a great deal about their outlook on life, their view of the world and their role in it. They think (as we all do when we ridicule our opponents in debate) that they have shown up the stupidity and the unbiblical nature of Jesus' beliefs. But Jesus reads Scripture differently, and his vision of God and of the world is radically different from theirs. In response, Jesus deconstructs their worldview and way of interpreting the Bible, and in doing so he draws attention to the vision that must drive bold Christian moral leadership.

Jesus focuses on marriage, a fundamental moral and social

institution rooted in creation. But here Jesus relates marriage to 'the people of this age'. The Sadducees, their outlook on life and their pattern of leadership are totally defined by this age – by marriage and family ties, and issues of status, honour, authority and inheritance. But, as discussed in the response to chapter 2, there is another age, which stands in sharp contrast to this present age, and a place in that age is in the gift of God. It is not tied to the social *status quo*, to biological reproduction or even to marriage. It is an age of resurrection from the dead, and those granted a place in it are children of God, children of the resurrection, who can no longer die.

This incident demonstrates Jesus' totally different outlook on the world. In the present age, death rules. This rule of death is evident in the Sadducees' obsession with such matters as continuing the name through marriage and offspring, which in turn leads people to hang on to everything they have, and to be defensive in the face of challenges and threats. It is evident too in the idolatries of our own age, which we identified earlier. Jesus' outlook is different, and so, even though people are out to kill him and the reality of death is already casting a dark shadow over him, even though he has nothing in terms of this present age to give him security and established authority, and even though his name is in danger of being blotted out from Israel, he will remain faithful to God's call to be the chosen leader of his chosen people.

Jesus' alternative outlook is rooted in the Scriptures where God reveals himself as the God of such sons of the resurrection as Abraham, Isaac and Jacob (Exod. 3:6), the true leaders and founders of the people of God. Death may have removed them from the social, cultural, historical worldly reality, but not from God, because 'to him all are alive' (Luke 20:38).

Here there is a challenge not just to the Sadducees but to all moral leaders. Our eyes are to be set on the God of the living and not on the world of death. The Sadducees – and we – are called humbly to give back to God what is God's (20:25 – a theme running through these chapters). They must therefore stop thinking they can ignore Jesus and the kingdom he proclaims and pass quietly from the scene, handing on what they have kept to those who follow them. Even death will not remove them from the sphere of God's rule, and ultimately God will decide whether or not we have our name carried on or blotted out. It is that vision of the age to come, of resurrection and of the kingdom of God that emboldened Jesus and that enables and empowers the radical moral leadership he lived out, disturbing the *status quo*.

In discussing symbolic actions by moral leaders, I mentioned the Berrigans, who were tried for using napalm to destroy military records. During their trial, the radical Christian lawyer William Stringfellow visited a nearby church to support his friends, despite being gravely ill and in great pain. There he addressed the congregation with these memorable words, which capture this Christlike hope in the age to come and trust in the God who raises the dead:

> Remember, now, that the State has only one power it can use against human beings: death. The State can persecute you, prosecute you, imprison you, exile you, execute you. All of these mean the same thing. The State can consign you to death. The grace of Jesus Christ in this life is that death fails. There is nothing the State can do to you, or to me, which we need fear.[10]

Taking Jesus as the moral of our story and pattern for moral leadership means learning and following lessons such as those we have found in these two passages from the Gospels. Such leadership will, like Jesus' leadership, be moral leadership not just for God's people but for the whole world. We must, however, remember that, like Jesus' leadership, faithful moral leadership of this form will often not be welcomed by the world and so its agenda and form must not be set by the world. Indeed, in the eyes of the world, it may well appear to end in failure. However, as Søren Kierkegaard reminds us –

To be sacrificed is ... as long as the world remains the world, a far greater achievement than to conquer; for the world is not so perfect that to be victorious in the world by adaptation to the world does not involve a dubious mixture of the world's paltriness. To be victorious in the world is like becoming something great in the world; ordinarily, to become something great in the world is a dubious matter, because the world is not so excellent that its judgment of greatness unequivocally has great significance – except as unconscious sarcasm.[11]

Conclusion

Let the conversation continue. For Christians, the central ethical issue is how are we to live out the coming of God's kingdom and do his will on earth as it is in heaven. Ethics is about the earthing of heaven. In the Lord's Prayer the doing of God's will on earth as it is done in heaven is a parallelism for the coming of the kingdom of God. Interpreting the kingdom of God has, in this book, been a matter of contention between Andrew and me. Oliver O'Donovan in *The Desire of the Nations* (page 82) summarizes the tension:

> That is why those who have asserted that a conception of Two Kingdoms is fundamental to Christian political thought have spoken truly, though at great risk of distorting the truth if they simply leave it at that. The unity of the kingdoms, we may say, is the heart of the Gospel, their duality is the pericardium. Proclaiming the unity of God's rule in Christ is the task of Christian witness; understanding the duality is the chief assistance rendered by Christian reflection.

'Proclaiming the unity of God's rule in Christ is the task of Christian witness.' This underlines the point that ethics and mission are inseparable. Those who are called to lead in the church and in the world cannot escape the moral complexities and ambiguities of our common life. Speaking very personally, whenever I am overwhelmed by moral dilemmas, I find myself retreating into that refuge of simply acknowledging the rule of Christ over my life and the whole world with the prayer 'Your kingdom come, your will be done on earth.' I say it over and over again, knowing that this was the heart of the message of Jesus.

This refuge is not a sound-proof cell with the door locked and the key removed. I can still hear the sounds of the questions; I know too that I will soon have to open the door and move into the world beyond and make decisions. But in that place of submission to the will of God there is a spiritual reality of sensing that God too wrestles with the obstructions and conflicts that impede the coming of his kingdom and therefore make it necessary for the disciple to pray and work towards the doing of his will on earth.

Christian moral leaders are given to prayer not because they will find in that sacred place the answers written instantly on the walls, but because there they will yield themselves to God who speaks in creation, history, Scripture and Jesus Christ.

The very act of yielding prayerfully to the will of God is in itself a coming of the kingdom, an inching closer of heaven to earth. Leaders are led by the Spirit to open the whole of their being to truth and grace. In spite of the grim realities in which many moral decisions have to be made, this prayerfulness paradoxically beckons us both to enter more fully into the dilemmas and to soar above in hope of a final and better day. As Gerard Manley Hopkins opined in his poem 'God's Grandeur',

> Because the Holy Ghost over the bent
> World broods with warm breast and ah! bright
>   wings.

The Rt Revd James Jones

Notes

1. Take me to your (moral) leader

1. Robert D. Putnam, *Bowling Alone: The Collapse and Revival of American Community* (London: Simon and Schuster, 2000).
2. Alan M. Suggate, 'Whither Anglican Social Ethics?', *Crucible* (April/June, 2001).
3. Ibid.
4. Ibid.
5. *The Sunday Telegraph*, 18 March 2001. Interview by Matthew d'Ancona.
6. Ibid.
7. Henry Washbourne, *A Practical View of the Prevailing Religious Systems of Professed Christians in the Higher and Middle Classes in This Country; Contrasted with Real Christianity* (London, 1836).
8. Thomas Price, in ibid., Preface.
9. William Wilberforce, in ibid., p. 266.
10. Ibid.
11. Paul Vallely (ed.), *New Politics: Catholic Social Teaching for the Twenty-first Century* (London: SCM, 1998).
12. Ibid., p. 154.
13. Robin Gill, *Moral Leadership in a Postmodern Age* (Edinburgh: T. & T. Clark, 1997).
14. Ibid.
15. Iris Murdoch, *Metaphysics as a Guide to Morals* (London: Penguin, 1993).
16. C. S. Lewis, *The Abolition of Man* (London: Geoffrey Bles, 1943).
17. Andrew Kirk, 'Care of the Environment', in *What is Mission?* (London: DLT, 1999), pp. 165–186.
18. Ibid., p. 174.
19. Pope John Paul II, *Evangelium Vitae* (Dublin: Veritas, 1995).
20. Oliver O'Donovan, *Resurrection and Moral Order* (1st ed.; Leicester: Apollos, 1986;), p. 20; cf. Anthony Harvey, *By What Authority?* (London: SCM, 2001).
21. Jacques Ellul, *The Technological Society* (London: Jonathan Cape, 1965). For more on Ellul see Andrew Goddard, *Living the Word, Resisting the World: the life and thought of Jacques Ellul* (Carlisle: Paternoster, 2002).

22. J. Ellul, *Propaganda: The Formation of Men's Attitudes* (New York: Knopf, 1965); Malcolm Muggeridge, *Christ and the Media* (London: Hodder & Stoughton, 1977).

23. Elizabeth Stuart, 'Dancing in the Spirit', in Tim Bradshaw (ed.), *The Way Forward? Homosexuality and the Church* (London: Hodder & Stoughton, 1997), p. 71.

2. The moral maze and the kingdom

1. Augustine, *Confessions* (London: Penguin, 1970).

2. Ibid.

3. Oliver O'Donovan, *Resurrection and Moral Order* (1st ed.; Leicester: Apollos, 1986).

4. Alan M. Suggate, *William Temple and Christian Social Ethics Today* (Edinburgh: T. & T. Clark, 1994).

5. O'Donovan, *Resurrection and Moral Order* , p. 15.

6. Ibid.

7. John A. T. Robinson, *Wrestling with 'Romans'* (London: SCM Press, 1979).

8. Alan M. Suggate, 'Whither Anglican Social Ethics?', *Crucible* (April/June, 2001).

9. James Jones, 'Is Conflict in the Church a Sign of Effective Mission?', Annual CMS Sermon, 2000, published by Church Missionary Society, 2001.

10. Paul Avis, *Church, State and the Establishment* (London: SPCK, 2001), p. 40.

11. Lesslie Newbigin, *The Other Side of 1984: Questions for the Churches* (Geneva: World Council of Churches, 1983), p. 39.

12. Karl Barth, Barmen Declaration, quoted in Eberhard Jungel, *Christ, Justice and Peace* (Edinburgh: T. & T. Clark, 1992), pp. xxii–xxiv.

13. Abraham Kuyper, quoted in Peter S. Heslam, *Creating a Christian Worldview: Abraham Kuyper's Lectures on Calvinism* (Carlisle: Paternoster, 1998), p. i.

14. O'Donovan, *Resurrection and Moral Order*, p. 15 (my emphasis).

15. R. T. France, *Divine Government: God's Kingship in the Gospel of Mark* (London: SPCK, 1990), p. 15.

16. An excellent recent example of such moral critique is Marva Dawn's *Powers, Weakness and the Tabernacling of God* (Grand Rapids: Eerdmans, 2001).

17. France, *Divine Government*, p. 15.

18. Stanley Hauerwas, *The Peaceable Kingdom* (London: SCM, 1983), p. 100.

19. This reading of Scripture is more fully developed in material I have prepared for the Bible and Politics module in Sarum College's Politics and Theology programme.

20. J. Hoffman, in *Williamson* vs *The Archbishops of Canterbury and York* (Chancery Division, 11 November 1994), cited in D. McClean, 'Establishment in a European Context', in N. Doe, M. Hill and R. Ombres (eds.), *English Canon Law: Essays in Honour of Bishop Eric Kemp* (Cardiff: University of Wales Press, 1998), p. 130.

21. From G. Bray (ed.), *The Anglican Canons 1529–1947* (Church of England Records Society, vol. 6) (Woodbridge, Suffolk: Boydell Press, Church of England Records Society, 1998), pp. 264–269.

22. Diarmaid MacCulloch, *Thomas Cranmer: A Life* (New Haven: Yale University Press, 1996), pp. 278–280.

3. The moral bridge over troubled waters

1. James Jones, 'Is Conflict in the Church a Sign of Effective Mission?', Annual CMS Sermon, 2000, published by Church Missionary Society, 2001.

2. Alan M. Suggate, *William Temple and Christian Social Ethics Today* (Edinburgh: T. & T. Clark, 1994).

3. Prince Charles, 'Respect for the Earth: A Royal View ...', Reith Lectures 2000, broadcast on BBC Radio 4 (text available on www.bbc.co.uk/radio4).

4. Richard Harries, 'Journey into the World Before Turning it Upside Down', in *Crucible* (April/June, 2001).

5. Ibid.

6. Ibid.

7. Ibid.

8. Ibid.

9. I have discussed some of this in relation to the difficult question of the church, homosexuality and gay culture in a Grove Ethics booklet – *God, Gentiles and Gay Christians: Acts 15 and Change in the Church*, Grove Ethics Series E121 (Cambridge: Grove Books, 2001).

10. For one approach to this see Stephen D. Long, *The Goodness of God: Theology, Church and the Social Order* (Brazos Press, 2001).

11. Dietrich Bonhoeffer, *Ethics* (London: SCM, 1955), p. 3.

12. N. T. Wright, *Jesus and the Victory of God* (London: SPCK, 1996), p. 443.

13. For a discussion about how this relates to evangelism today see Graham Tomlin, *The Provocative Church* (SPCK: London, 2002); Rodney Clapp, *A Peculiar People: The Church as Culture in a Post-Christian Society* (Downers Grove: IVP, 1996).

14. J. K. Rowling, *Harry Potter and the Chamber of Secrets* (London: Bloomsbury, 1998), p. 245. I have discussed this further in 'Harry Potter and the Quest for Virtue', *Anvil* 18.3 (2001), pp. 181–192.

4. The moral of this story? Jesus

1. Iris Murdoch, *Metaphysics as a Guide to Morals* (London: Penguin, 1993), p. 352.
2. Ibid., p. 368.
3. Wilhelm Hermann, quoted in Wolfhart Pannenberg, *Ethics* (Philadelphia: Westminster Press, 1981), p. 58.
4. Murdoch, *Metaphysics as a Guide to Morals*, p. 368.
5. John Howard Yoder.
6. Alan M. Suggate, 'Whither Anglican Social Ethics?', *Crucible* (April/June, 2001).
7. Ibid.
8. Will Self, interviewed by Steve Turner, 'Getting a Fix', *Third Way*, vol. no. 24(5) (July, 2001).
9. Stanley Hauerwas, quoted by W. Cavanaugh, 'Stan the Man: A Thoroughly Biased Account of a Completely Unobjective Person', in *The Hauerwas Reader* (Durham, NC: Duke University Press, 2001), p. 29.
10. William Stringfellow, *A Second Birthday* (New York: Doubleday, 1970), p. 133. The best introduction to Stringfellow's work is Bill Wylie Kellerman (ed.), *A Keeper of the Word: Selected Writings of William Stringfellow* (Grand Rapids: Eerdmans, 1994).
11. Quotation from Kierkegaard, *Works of Love* (Hong & Hong, 1962), p. 288. Quoted in Kathryn Tanner, *Jesus Humanity and the Trinity* (Edinburgh: T. & T. Clark, 2002), p. 124.